C000229262

WWW.DIYTOOLKIT.ORG

Development Impact & You

PRACTICAL TOOLS TO TRIGGER & SUPPORT SOCIAL INNOVATION

DIY PRODUCTION TEAM: **Theo Keane, Brenton Caffin, Michael Soto** (Nesta) + **Ayush Chauhan, Rikta Krishnaswamy** (Quicksand) + **Geke van Dijk, Megha Wadhawan** (STBY)

WITH MANY KIND CONTRIBUTIONS FROM PEOPLE & ORGANISATIONS AROUND THE WORLD

Aakash Sethi
Quest Alliance

Aaron Good
Innoweave

Adam Groves
One World

Adam Pike
Young Philanthropy

Aditya Dev Sood & Ekta Ohri
Center for Knowledge Societies

Andreas Karpati
UNDP Uzbekistan

Annemarie Naylor
Common Futures

Anusuya Banerjee
Jameel Poverty Action Lab

Arun Patre
SELCO Incubation Centre

Arvind Lodaya
Independent Design Practitioner

Ashmeet Kapoor
ISayOrganic

Ben Gallagher
Nike Foundation

Ben Reason
LiveWork

Chris Albon & Angela Oduor
Ushahidi

Chris Vanstone & Adele Liddle
TACSI

Christopher Fabian
Unicef Innovation

Dan Berelowitz
International Centre for Social Franchising

Dan Radcliff
Bill and Melinda Gates Foundation

Deborah Szebeko
ThinkPublic

Dianne Denton
UNESCO

Faith Gonsalves
Music Basti

Faustina Gomez
Technology and Action for Rural Advancement

Geetanjali Kumar
Development Alternatives

George Hodge
UNDP Armenia

Giulio Quaggiotto
UNDP Europe and the CIS

Heather Leson
Open Knowledge Foundation

Jack Graham
Year Here

Jacqueline Simmons
Teachers College Columbia University

Jennie Winhall
Participle

Joel Adriance
International Youth Foundation

John Owrid
IndexB

Jon Huggett
Social Innovation Exchange

Jonathan Wong
DFID

Karthik Chauhan
Clinton Health Initiative

Kate Chapman
Humanitarian Open Street Map

Kate Wareing
Oxfam, Programme Policy

Katharine Hibbert
Dot Dot Dot Property

Kristine Hovhannisyan
Oxfam Armenia

Lejla Sadiku
UNDP Kosovo

Louise Pulford
Social Innovation Exchange

Lucy Kimbell
Said Business School

Lucy McNab
Ministry of Stories

Maksym Klyuchar
UNDP Ukraine

Marc Stickdorn
This is Service Design Thinking

Matthew McStravick
HackneyShares

Megha Bhagat
NASSCOM Foundation

Nathan Cooke, Marielle Schweikhart, Simon Dixon, Miranda Lewis &Dennis Onyango
Sanergy

Nikita Dagar
Digital Green

Paula Dib
Trans.forma

Paula Gutierrez
The Hub Bogota

Pukar Malla
World Bank

Renata Mendes
SBCSol

Rikin Gandhi
Digital Green

Roger Swartz
Positive Deviance Initiative

Satbir Singh
Human Rights Initiative

Sean Lowrie
Start Network

Sean Miller
Nonon

Sergio Rivas
ACDI / VOCA

Shahina Bahar
British Red Cross

Subbiah Krishnaswamy & Ravi Kommuri
Family Health International 360

Sujaya rathi & Jay Asundi
Center for Study of Science, Technology and Ploicy

Tarun Markose
Teemac

Thea Aldrich
Random Hacks of Kindness

Urvashi Aneja
Center for Global Governance and Policy, JSIA

Will Norman
The Young Foundation

Yi Wei
iDe Cambodia

This work is ©Nesta licensed under the Creative Commons Attribution-NonCommercial-ShareAlike 4.0 International Licence.
To view a copy of the licence, visit http://creativecommons.org/licenses/by-nc-sa/4.0/

SUPPORTED BY

This is a toolkit on how to invent, adopt or adapt ideas that can deliver better results.

This is a toolkit on how to invent, adopt or adapt ideas that can deliver better results. It's quick to use, simple to apply, and designed to help busy people working in development. It draws on a study of many hundreds of tools currently being used - here we have included only the ones which practitioners found most useful.

The tools are not coming out of thin air. Many of them are well documented and have been widely used in other sectors. In that sense this toolkit is standing on the shoulders of giants, and we are happy to acknowledge that.

All the tool descriptions include a key reference, so it is easy to trace back their origins and dive deeper into other publications about their application.

AN INITIATIVE OF

Nesta...

MADE POSSIBLE BY

DESIGNED BY

..STBY...

I want to……

look ahead

to understand what I need to do to bring my idea to life
INNOVATION FLOWCHART

by defining the outcomes from my work
EVIDENCE PLANNING

develop a clear plan

by evaluating how I am doing and what my options are
SWOT ANALYSIS

on how to grow my idea into something bigger
BUSINESS MODEL CANVAS

for working with other groups that have the same vision as me
BUILDING PARTNERSHIPS MAP

by improving upon what I've done before
LEARNING LOOP

clarify my priorities

by learning from first hand experiences
EXPERIENCE TOUR

by focusing on key critical issues
PROBLEM DEFINITION

by breaking down a complex issue
CAUSES DIAGRAM

by defining my goals and the path to reach them
THEORY OF CHANGE

collect input from others

by observing and learning from everyday life
PEOPLE SHADOWING

in a conversation that uncovers their perspective
INTERVIEW GUIDE

by getting to the heart of what motivates people
QUESTION LADDER

to ensure my work is relevant to the people I'm working for
STORYWORLD

know the people I'm working with

by clarifying relationships between stakeholders
PEOPLE & CONNECTIONS MAP
15

by better defining who I am trying to reach
TARGET GROUP
16

by visualising their key characteristics
PERSONAS
17

by defining how my offering is new to them
PROMISES & POTENTIAL MAP
18

generate new ideas

by working together with people who experience and solve problems
CREATIVE WORKSHOP
19

by thinking differently
FAST IDEA GENERATOR
20

by framing a constructive discussion with my team
THINKING HATS
21

by aligning our work based on shared values
VALUE MAPPING
22

test & improve

by understanding what is most effective in my work
IMPROVEMENT TRIGGERS
23

by collecting useful feedback on my work at different phases
PROTOTYPE TESTING PLAN
24

by creating an overview of how I engage with my stakeholders
EXPERIENCE MAP
25

by crafting a detailed overview of our operations and resources
BLUEPRINT
26

sustain & implement

by better engaging people that can benefit from my work
MARKETING MIX
27

by executing my plan without being overwhelmed
CRITICAL TASKS LIST
28

by launching or growing what I do
BUSINESS PLAN
29

while exploring different ways of increasing the scale of my work
SCALING PLAN
30

Structuring a master plan to redesign and build inclusive sanitation facilities in urban slums in India.

I want to look ahead to understand what I need to do to bring my idea to life

INNOVATION FLOWCHART

INSPIRED BY
Nesta (2013) Innovation Flowchart.

LEVEL OF INVOLVEMENT

MORE COMPLEX TOOL that should ideally be done over a few days. Given the strategic nature of the inputs/outputs, this needs consultations with seniors, peers and ideally needs to be revised after a first pass.

INNOVATION FLOWCHART

What is it & why should I do it?

The **Innovation Flowchart** gives a detailed overview of the various stages in an innovation process, listing the activities, requirements and goals of each stage. These include an overview of the different people, skills, activities and finances that a project or an organisation might need in order to succeed. The structured overview this tool provides, helps review where you are in the process, and to organise the next steps in your work.

This tool helps you to spot opportunities for growth by helping you understand which resources to focus on. You can see this by checking where you are in the process and whether you have thought of all the aspects that need consideration.

? HOW TO USE IT

The worksheet gives an overview of the various stages in an innovation process, and it lists stage by stage the activities, requirements and goals of each stage. Use this overview to check where you are in the process, and whether you have thought of all the aspects that need consideration. This check may help you to identify what things need special attention. The overview comes with a handy reference to the tools and activities that can support you in each stage.

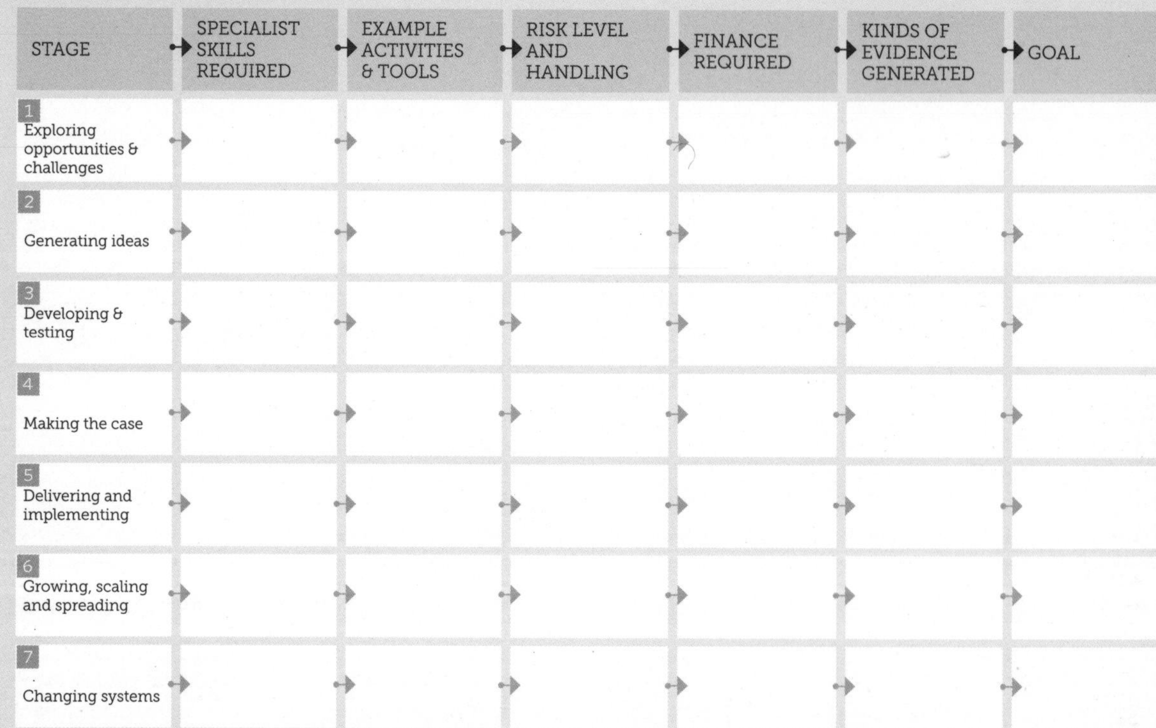

STAGE	SPECIALIST SKILLS REQUIRED	EXAMPLE ACTIVITIES & TOOLS	RISK LEVEL AND HANDLING	FINANCE REQUIRED	KINDS OF EVIDENCE GENERATED	GOAL
1 Exploring opportunities & challenges						
2 Generating ideas						
3 Developing & testing						
4 Making the case						
5 Delivering and implementing						
6 Growing, scaling and spreading						
7 Changing systems						

I want to look ahead
to understand what I need to do to bring my idea to life

INNOVATION FLOWCHART

STAGE	SPECIALIST SKILLS REQUIRED	EXAMPLE ACTIVITIES & TOOLS	RISK LEVEL AND HANDLING	FINANCE REQUIRED	KINDS OF EVIDENCE GENERATED	GOAL
1 Exploring opportunities & challenges	Research for exploratory work	SWOT Analysis Problem Definition Causes Diagram	Low risk of failure but clear decisions should be taken about how to act on insights	Grants	Insights derived from formal research and informal knowledge gathering	A well understood and clearly defined problem or opportunity
2 Generating ideas	Ideation and facilitation of creative thinking	Thinking Hats Fast Idea Generator Creative Workshop	High failure rate should be an explicit expectation, visible senior leadership essential	Usually grants, occasionally convertible	A clear account of change or likely causation, supported-but not overly constrained by evidence	An idea or set of ideas to develop and test
3 Developing & testing	Mix of design and implementation skills	Experience Map Prototype Testing Plan Improvement Triggers	High failure rate should be an explicit expectation, visible senior leadership essential	Grants, convertible grants/loans	A stronger case with cost and benefit projections developed through practical trials and experiments, involving potential users	Demonstration that the idea works, or evidence to support a reworking of the idea
4 Making the case	Business development and evaluation	Blueprint Promises & Potential Map Business Model Canvas	Prepare to adapt approach, based on evaluation results and user feedback	Grant funding or funding out of investment	A stronger case with cost and benefit projections developed through practical trials and experiments, involving potential users	Clarity about what warrants implementation and funding
5 Delivering and implementing	Strong leadership, management, implementation skills	Critical Tasks List Learning Loop Target Group	Prepare for some adaptation to implementation	Programme funds, equity, loans, grants	A robust and detailed case developed through formal evaluation and evidence gathering - use of a control group to isolate impact	An implemented and sustainable innovation
6 Growing, scaling and spreading	Strong leadership, management, implementation skills	Scaling Plan Business Plan Marketing Mix	Fidelity assessments may be important, strong capacity needed to ensure transfer of practice	Equity loans, payment by results, social impact bonds	Evidence derived from evaluations in multiple sites, and independently run randomised control trials	Innovation or impact at scale
7 Changing systems	Strong leadership and management, Identification and training of new leaders and teams	Building Partnerships Map Evidence Planning	Map potential unintended effects	Multiple financial systems requiring potential re-wiring possible outcome-based funding	New definitions of and measures for efficiency and impact created	A transformation in the way we do things

Planning ahead on with students at their university on social design projects.

I want to look ahead by defining the outcomes from my work

EVIDENCE PLANNING

INSPIRED BY
Nesta (2009) Worksheet 2b: Evidence Modelling. In: Creative Enterprise Toolkit.

LEVEL OF INVOLVEMENT

REQUIRES SOME DIALOGUE with colleagues/peers. Plan for some time to interact and fill out in collaboration over a day maybe.

What is it & why should I do it?

Why do you do what you do? The **Evidence Planning** tool is a quick way to help articulate and improve what you are trying to accomplish. It gives you an easy way to define and share what you're trying to do, and the assumptions and evidence upon which this is based. By making you think more broadly about your work's effect on target beneficiaries, society and other organisations, Evidence Planning helps you construct an evidence-based case for the impact you want to have.

The Evidence Planning tool provides a structured way to project the effects of your activities onto the future. This will help you reflect on what you may want to change or retain. This tool also helps to highlight at an early stage any potential problems or easy to make mistakes.

HOW TO USE IT

Start by filling out the key focus for your work or organisation in the middle of the worksheet. Then use the questions in the four quadrants to reflect on what your key focus enhances, replaces or even limits. Think of changes that your work would make in the sector, on other public and private bodies, as well as the effect it would have on society. This offers you a window to consider the impact your work may have.

Look at the key aspects from diverse points of view. While filling out the four quadrants think of:

- The wider world. (Think as big as possible.)
- Your particular field or area of interest. (eg. How it might impact current practices)
- Your beneficiaries (What benefits will it bring them?)
- Yourself (What impact could it have on your work/life?)

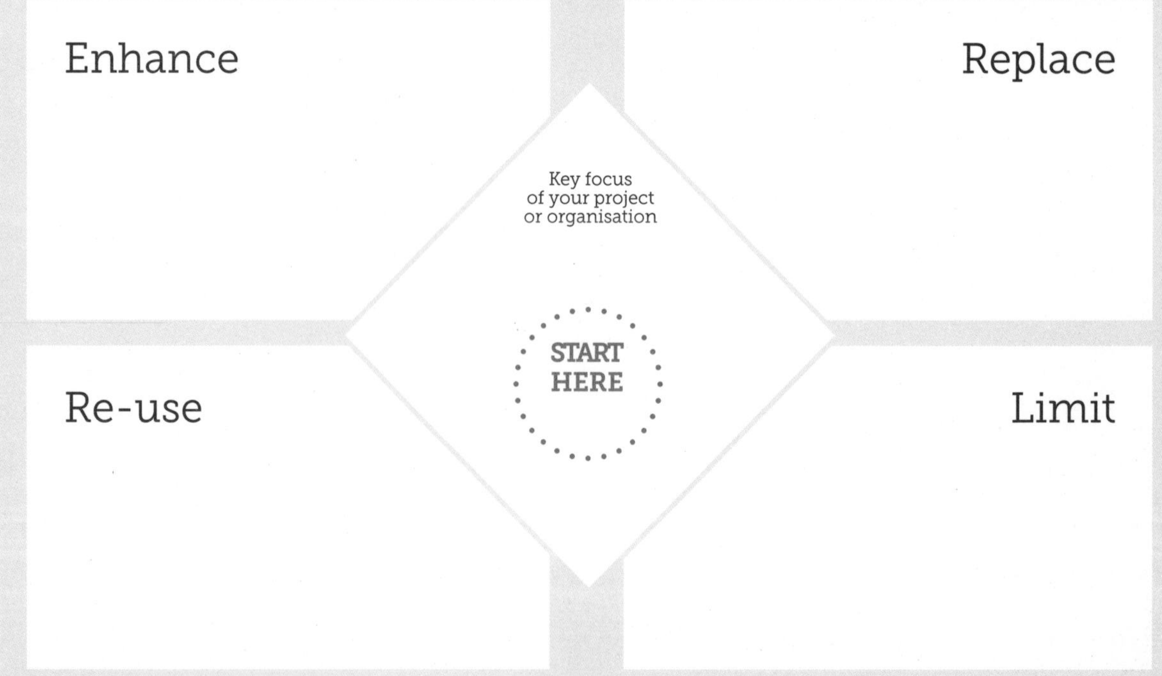

I want to look ahead
by defining the outcomes from my work

EVIDENCE PLANNING

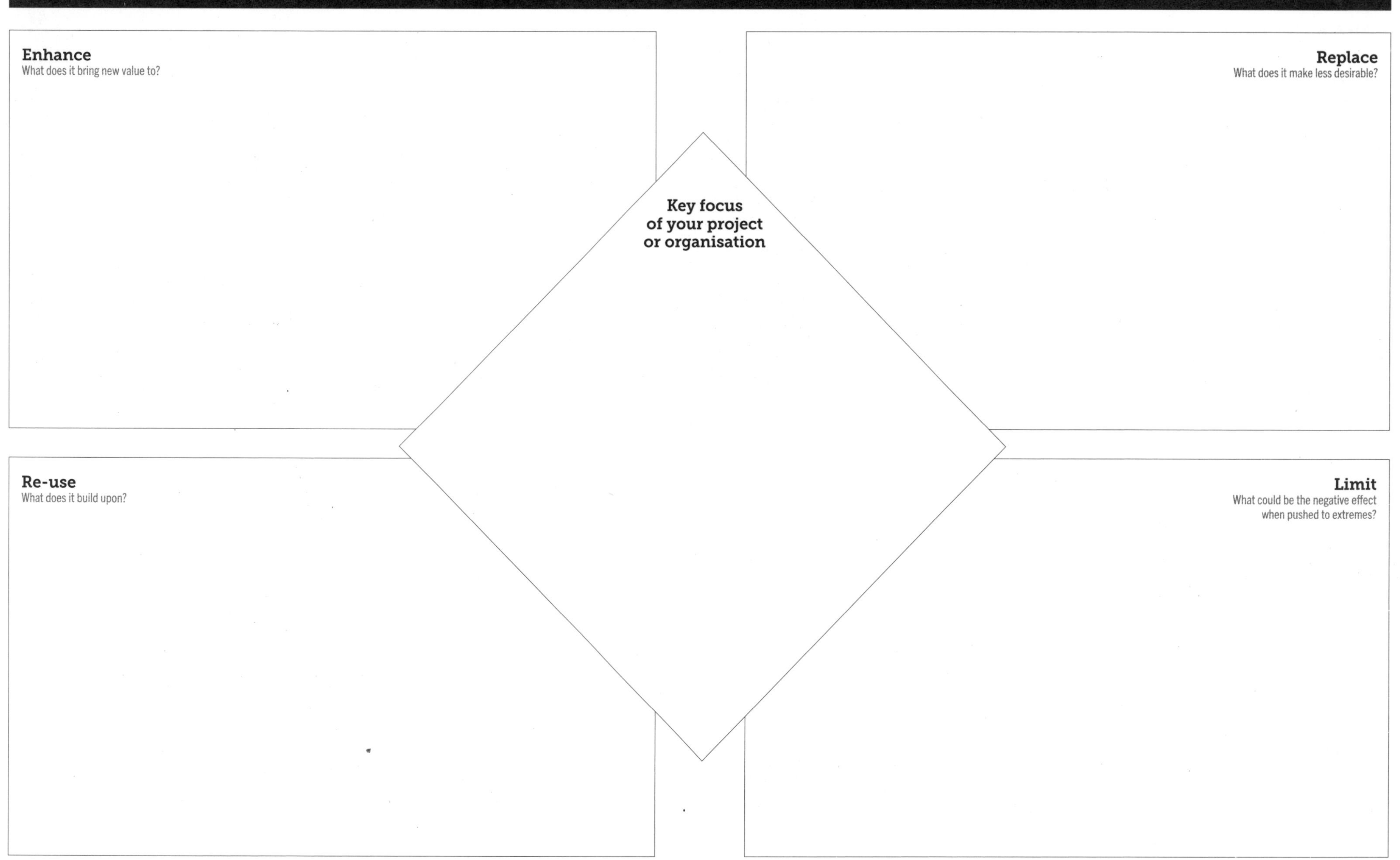

 DIY

CASE STUDY

TOOL USED: EVIDENCE PLANNING

ORGANISATION: UNDP KOSOVO

COUNTRY: KOSOVO

SECTOR: LOCAL GOVERNANCE

ROLE: PROJECT MANAGER, SOCIAL MEDIA FOR INNOVATIVE LOCAL EMPOWERMENT

CONTACT PERSON: LEJLA SADIKU

EMAIL: LEJLA.SADIKU@UNDP.ORG

FURTHER INFORMATION: HTTP://UNDP.AKVOAPP.ORG/FR/PROJECT/1338/

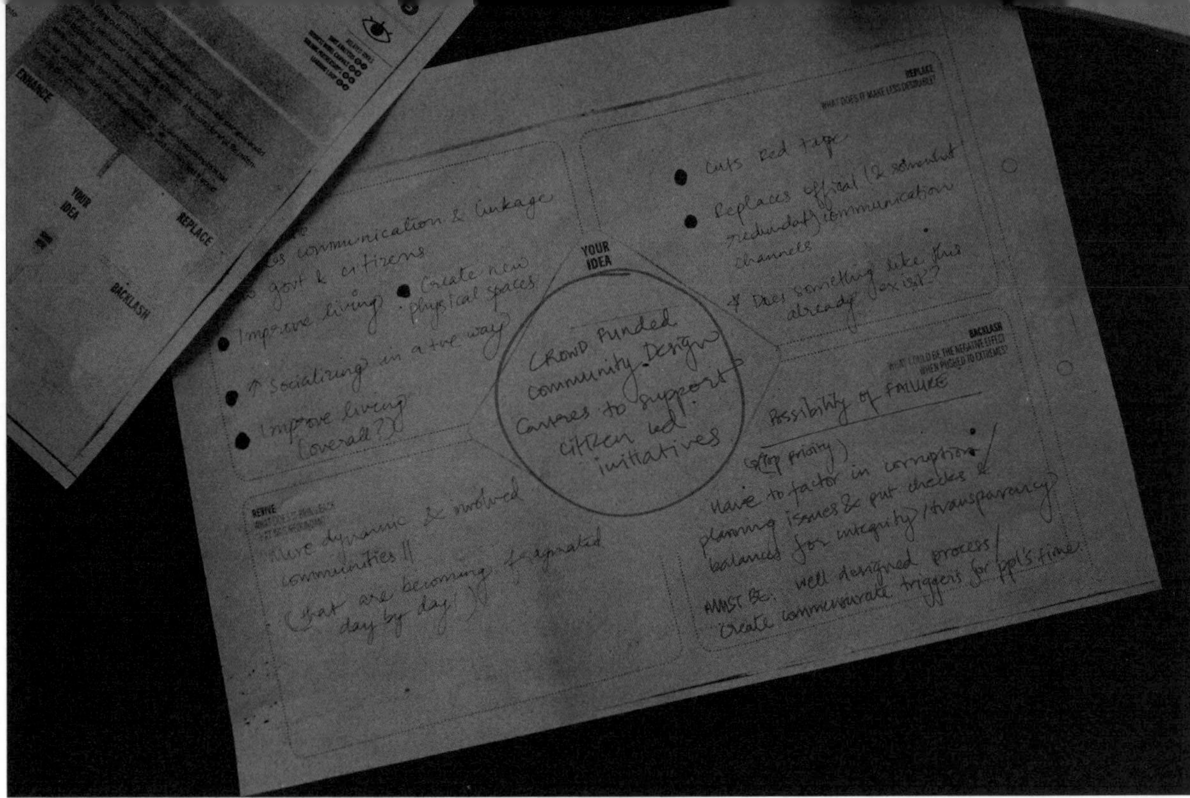

KEY OUTCOMES FROM THE EVIDENCE PLANNING WORKSHOP WITH DESIGN AND ARCHITECTURE STUDENTS.

We are looking to scope Community Design Centres that adopt crowd-funding mechanisms to support citizen led initiatives.

THIS SYSTEM WOULD INVOLVE:

- Citizen body proposals for community development being registered on a central crowd-funding site.
- Mobilising architecture and design students with members of the municipality government to design a product or solution in partnership, post funding.

WHY WE USED THE TOOL:

This project is currently at an early concept stage and we are trying to recruit members of our target audience. We wanted to stretch our thinking to look at and test our idea from a different perspective.

HOW WE USED THE TOOL:

We presented the project and its objectives to a group of 60-70 people at the Department for Design, Public University in Pristina. It was a big group and we wanted to capture as much feedback as possible. The students that attended the workshop deliberated what this project could mean for their local community and we were able to get some really important inputs from our key stakeholders.

It helped us identify triggers for ensuring engagement with different community members (for example art students are more interested in projects related to aesthetics).

It emphasised the need for a well designed process for engagement. This is extremely crucial when you are asking people to spare pro-bono time and effort.

RESULTS OF USING THE TOOL:

Thanks to this activity, our team has initiated significant momentum for the project. This exercise was very useful in two aspects:

- It helped us identify triggers for ensuring engagement with different community members (for example art students are more interested in projects related to aesthetics).
- It emphasised the need for a well designed process for engagement. This is extremely crucial when you are asking people to spare pro-bono time and effort.

CASE STUDY

TOOL USED: EVIDENCE PLANNING, PROBLEM DEFINITION

ORGANISATION: TEEMAC

COUNTRY: INDIA

SECTOR: EDUCATION

ROLE: DIRECTOR

CONTACT PERSON: TARUN MARKOSE

EMAIL: TARUNMARKOSE@GMAIL.COM

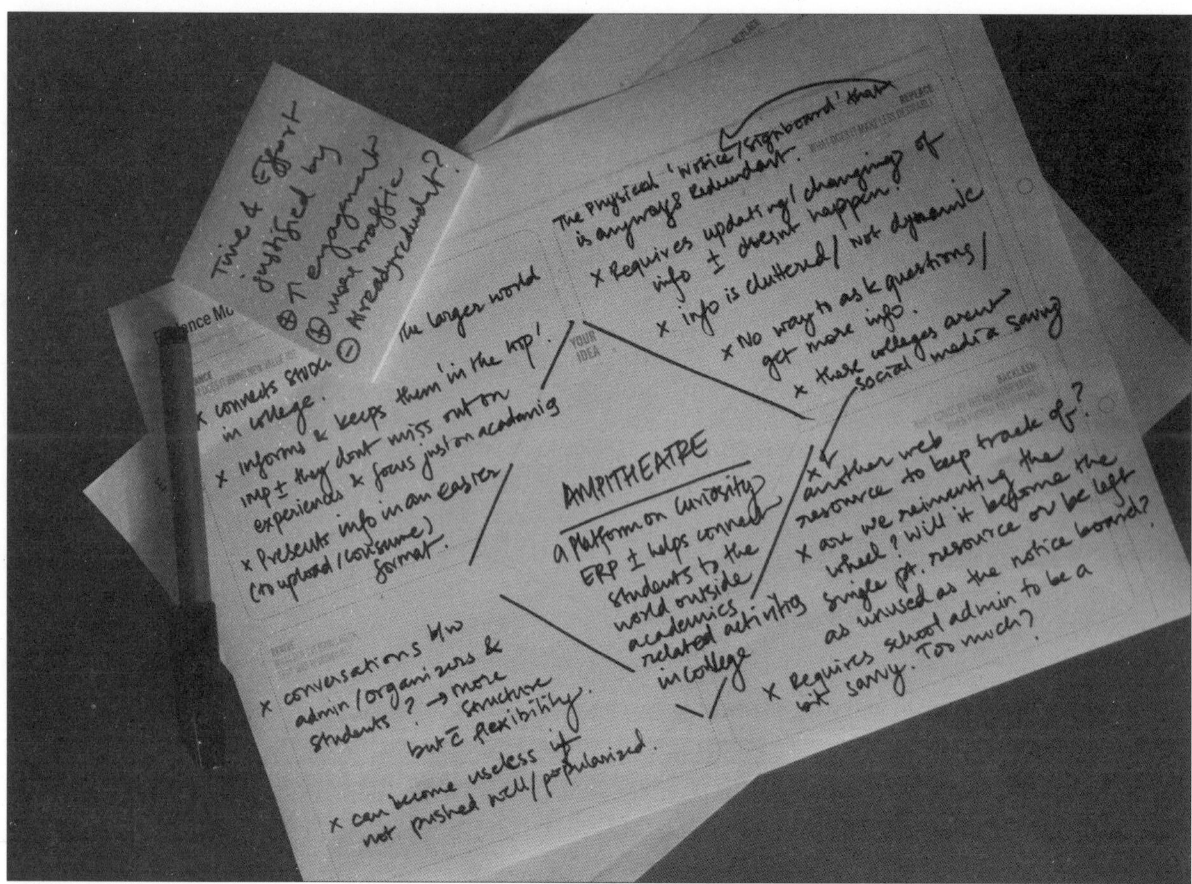

A PICTURE OF THE WORKSHEET THAT CULMINATED OUT OF THE TEAM DISCUSSION.

Teemac works with educational institutions creating products to help them modernise practices through an enterprise resource planning (ERP) platform called Curiosity, that we've developed in collaboration with pioneering educators.

We are currently working on a feature called Amphitheater which connects college students to extra curricular activities and events happening in their college.

Right now most of the institutions we work with have an age-old bulletin board with ad-hoc, outdated information and no one point where students or college admin can access or update information.

THE TEAM AT TEEMAC IS A MIX OF PEOPLE FROM DOMAINS OF WEB DEVELOPMENT, BUSINESS AND USER EXPERIENCE DESIGN.

WHY WE USED THE TOOL:

We had realised that we are very idealistic when it comes to building features within the Curiosity platform. We usually follow our gut instinct, even when the institutions do not see an explicit value in them. For a change, we thought we would adopt a more evidence based approach before we start building the Amphitheater feature.

We used a combination of Problem Definition and Evidence Planning. This was to both define and create a logical evidence based plan for the problem we are trying to solve.

HOW WE USED THE TOOL:

Two of my team mates and I printed out the worksheets and sat around a table with our notes and thoughts. The Problem Definition tool only helped us articulate what we already knew. The most interesting part was the last question "Can you think of this problem in a different way? Can you reframe it?" Sometimes you look at a problem and try solve it very linearly, this question helped us deliberate if there was a different way of looking at the problem itself.

The Evidence Planning Worksheet was surprisingly interesting. When we started filling it out, we realised that we weren't convinced of the evidence backing the solution as well as the impact it could create. We ended up slightly confused about the direction and found ourselves arguing amongst each other. We haven't found the answers yet, but its still definitely a positive outcome.

RESULTS OF USING THE TOOL:

This activity made us doubt something that we were absolutely sure of creating. It helped us introspect and rethink an entire system we were going to create based on our intuition. It was a good exercise because it helped us achieve a deeper understanding of what we were trying to do.

It helped us introspect and rethink an entire system we were going to create based on our intuition.

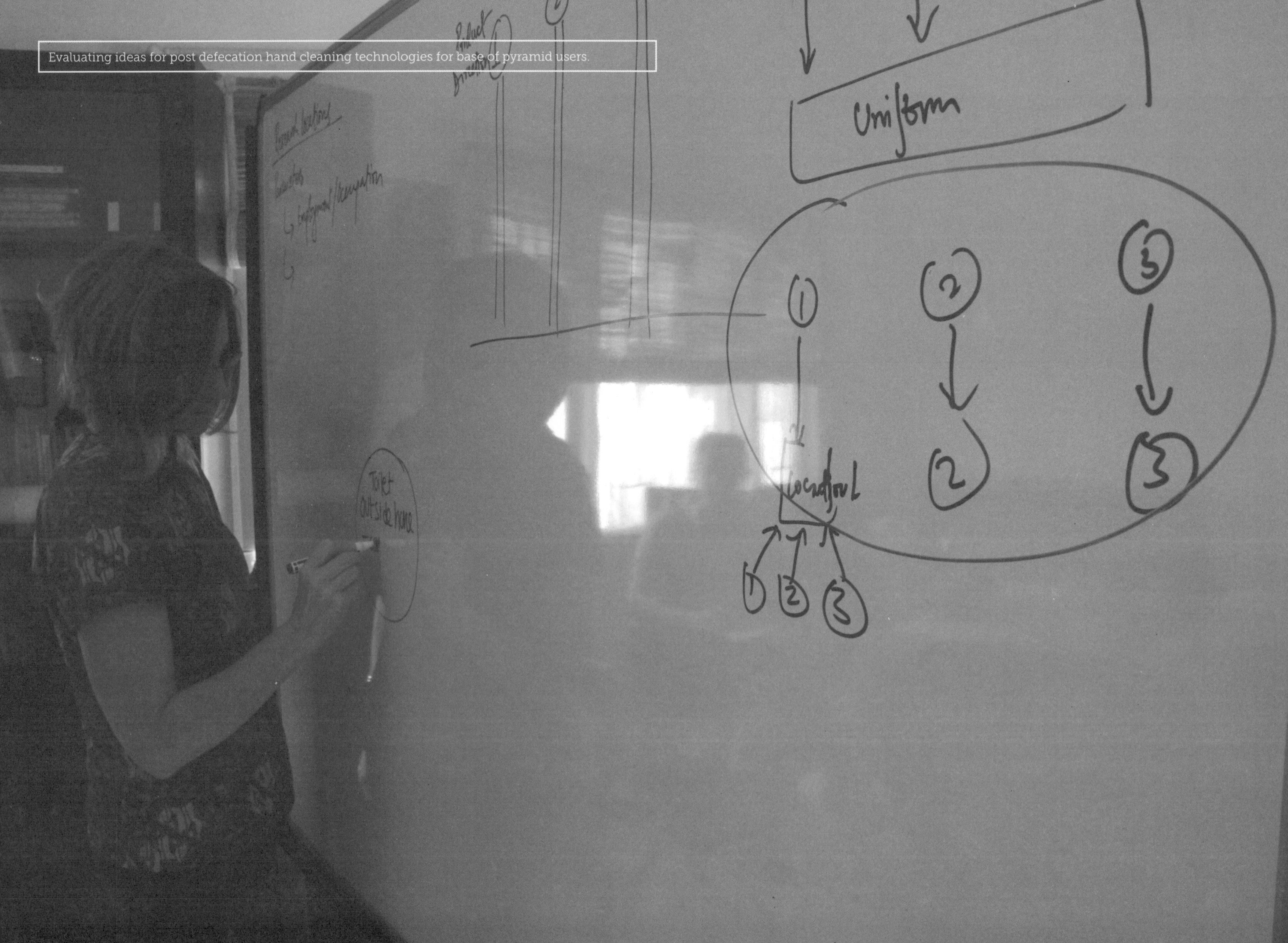

Evaluating ideas for post defecation hand cleaning technologies for base of pyramid users.

I want to develop a clear plan by evaluating how I am doing and what my options are

SWOT ANALYSIS

INSPIRED BY
MindTools (1996) SWOT Analysis.

LEVEL OF INVOLVEMENT

REQUIRES SOME DIALOGUE with colleagues/peers. Plan for some time to interact and fill out in collaboration over a day maybe.

SWOT ANALYSIS

What is it & why should I do it?

SWOT stands for Strengths, Weaknesses, Opportunities and Threats. A **SWOT Analysis** can be carried out for a specific project, organisation or even a whole sector. This analysis leads to a richer understanding of what the project or organisation can offer, the key weaknesses that need to be worked upon in order to succeed, and where to bring in external partners for assistance.

Completing a SWOT Analysis involves identifying and mapping the internal and external factors that are assisting or hindering you in achieving your goal. The SWOT Analysis provides a good framework for reviewing current strategies and directions, or even to test an idea while exploring solutions. It is particularly helpful to do a SWOT Analysis before the start of a project.

? HOW TO USE IT

A SWOT Analysis can be made for an entire organisation, but also for individual departments, programmes or even projects. Complete each of the quadrants in the worksheet according to what you see as your or your organisation's strengths and weaknesses as well as the external opportunities and threats that may help or hinder you.

Here are some tips to help you further:

Be prepared: Get your facts and figures in place before you do the analysis.

Be comprehensive: Include all details, from the smallest ones (e.g. for issues at the most micro level like discussions in your team) to large ones (e.g. for new government regulation) that can impact your work.

Be self-critical: SWOT Analysis is there to stimulate critical reflection, not just to please yourself and/or others. Be open and don't get defensive. It is normal to have weaknesses as well as strengths, and to see both threats and opportunities. Sometimes talking about weaknesses or threats can even help you recognise strengths and opportunities.

Test your analysis with others: Include others or maybe even ask an outsider (like your partner organisation) to do the same exercise and compare their views with your findings.

Repeat the analysis: As you go on with your work, new learnings and factors are bound to come up. Re-visit the SWOT Analysis to align your work and its course once every quarter or twice a year.

Use it as a guide: Don't rely on SWOT too much – it's a guide that can help scope the way for further development.

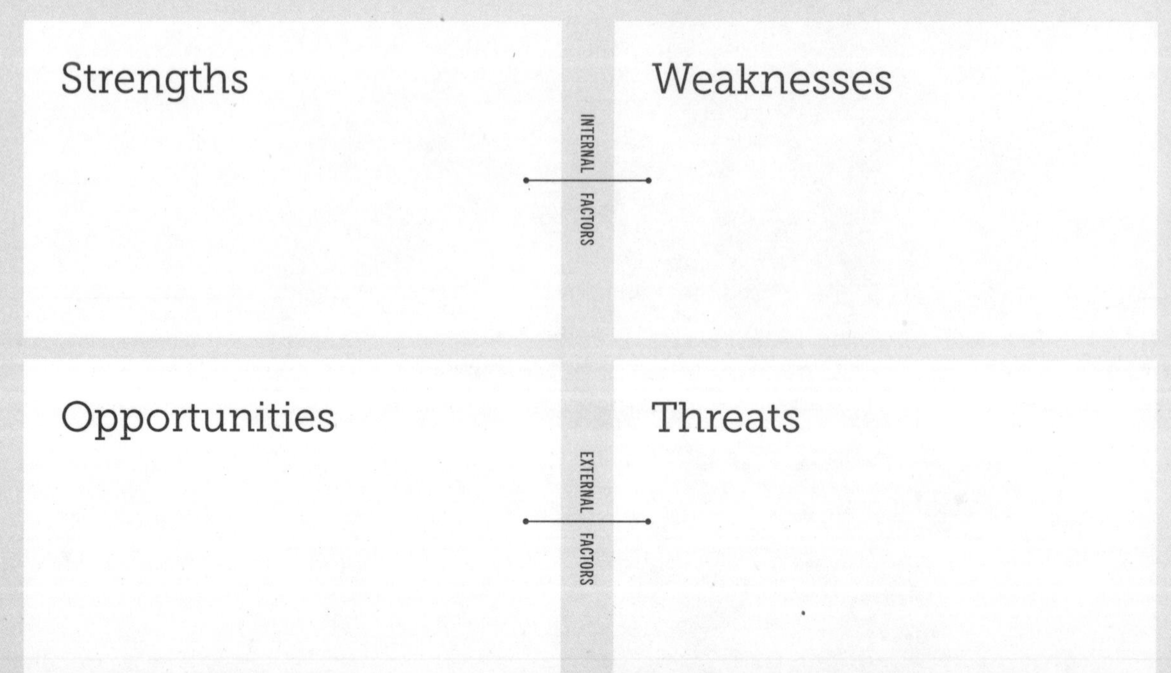

I want to develop a clear plan
by evaluating how I am doing and what my options are

SWOT ANALYSIS

Strengths
What do you do better than anyone else?
What makes you unique?
What unique or lowest-cost resources can you draw upon that others can't?
What do people in your market see as your strengths?

INTERNAL FACTORS

Weaknesses
What could you improve?
What should you avoid?
What are things that users might see as weaknesses?

Opportunities
Do people have a need?
Do people prefer something else?
Are there any changes in technology?
Are there changes in government policy?

EXTERNAL FACTORS

Threats
What challenges do you face?
What are your competitors doing?
Is changing technology making things difficult?
Is there an issue with finances?

Trying out different business models along with the team, to work out the most suitable one.

Global Service Jam London 2013

I want to develop a clear plan on how to grow my idea into something bigger

BUSINESS MODEL CANVAS

CREATED BY
Osterwalder A., Pigneur Y (2010) Business Model Generation

LEVEL OF INVOLVEMENT

MORE COMPLEX TOOL that should ideally be done over a few days. Given the strategic nature of the inputs/outputs, this needs consultations with seniors, peers and ideally needs to be revised after a first pass.

What is it & why should I do it?

The **Business Model Canvas** is a one page overview that lays out both what you do (or want to do), and how you go about doing it; enabling structured conversations around management and strategy by laying out the crucial activities and challenges involved with your initiative and how they relate to each other. This visual format, first introduced by Osterwalder and Pigneur, is useful for both existing and new organisations and businesses. Existing programmes can develop new initiatives and identify opportunities while becoming more efficient by illustrating potential trade-offs and aligning activities. New programmes can use it to plan and work out how to make their offering real.

The individual elements prompt thoughts within the separate activities or resources, while the capability to have the complete overview encourages fresh perspectives and ideas about how those pieces fit together. This structure also helps to keep group discussions more focused and bring everyone onto the same page.

HOW TO USE IT

To make a Business Model Canvas, the easiest way to start is by filling out what you do. This helps keep the focus on your main goal as you fill out the other building blocks of the canvas. From there you can build on that goal and see how it can be achieved by adding details about the other activities and resources you have.

Start from a blank canvas and add notes with keywords to each building block of the canvas. If you use 'sticky notes' for this, you can move ideas around as you fill out each building block in the canvas. You may want to colour-code elements related to a specific client segment.

However, be careful not to fall in love with your first idea and instead sketch out alternative business models for the same product, service, or technology.

You could even practice and learn new ways of doing things by mapping out new/innovative business models that you admire or come across.

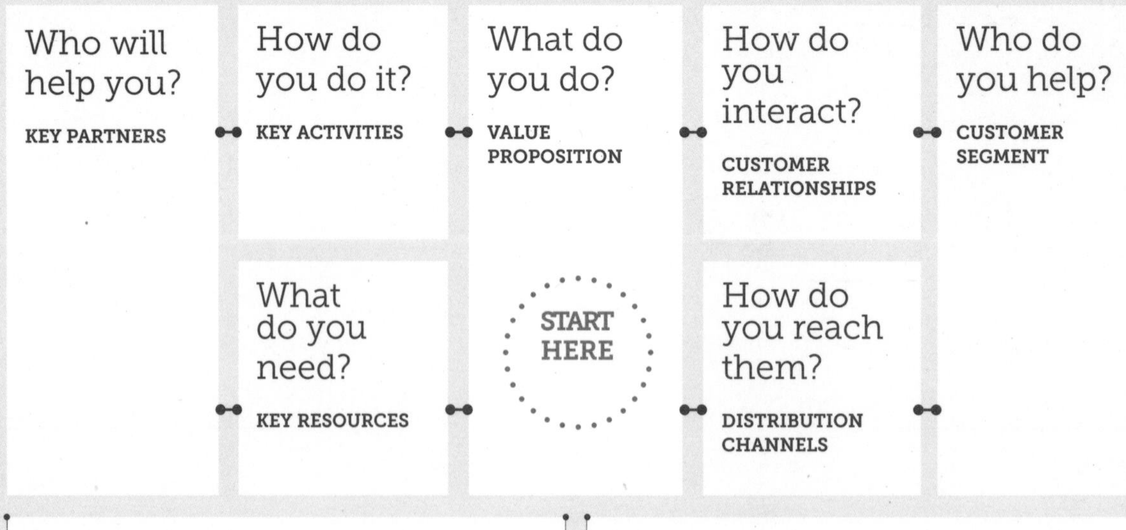

I want to develop a clear plan
on how to grow my idea into something bigger

BUSINESS MODEL CANVAS

Who will help you?
KEY PARTNERS

Who are your key partners/suppliers?
What are the most important motivations for the partnerships?

How do you do it?
KEY ACTIVITIES

What key activities does your value proposition require?
What activities are most important for your distribution channels, customer relationships, revenue streams etc?

What do you need?
KEY RESOURCES

What key resources does your value proposition require?

What do you do?
VALUE PROPOSITION

What core value do you deliver to your audience?
Which needs are you satisfying?

How do you interact?
AUDIENCE RELATIONSHIPS

What relationship does the target audience expect you to establish?
How can you integrate that into your work in terms of cost and format?

How do you reach them?
DISTRIBUTION CHANNELS

Through which channel does your audience want to be reached?
Which channels work best? How much do they cost?
How can they be integrated into your and your audiences routines?

Who do you help?
AUDIENCE SEGMENTS

Which groups are you creating value for?
Who is your most important audience?

What will it cost?
COST STRUCTURE

What are the most important costs in your work?
Which key resources/ activities are most expensive?

How much will you make?
REVENUE STREAM

For what value are your audiences willing to pay?
What and how do they recently pay? How would they prefer to pay?
How much does every revenue stream contribute to the overall revenues?

Project planning workshop with various levels of partners working on financial inclusion.

I want to develop a clear plan for working with other groups that have the same vision as me.

BUILDING PARTNERSHIPS MAP

INSPIRED BY
Tennyson R. (2003) 12 Phases in the Partnering Process, p4. In: The Partnering Toolbook.

LEVEL OF INVOLVEMENT

MORE COMPLEX TOOL that should ideally be done over a few days. Given the strategic nature of the inputs/outputs, this needs consultations with seniors, peers and ideally needs to be revised after a first pass.

BUILDING PARTNERSHIPS MAP

What is it & why should I do it?

Many complex problems have several different yet related causes and effects - with several organisations from different sectors trying to solve things individually. With many organisations having limited resources, forming partnerships is a good approach to not only increase capability, but also your reach. Partnerships help build a common understanding, and harness the knowledge which might be spread across various different perspectives.

Building partnerships takes a lot of effort from all those involved. It often takes a considerable investment of time to build the high quality working relationships that underpin effective collaboration. The **Building Partnerships Map** breaks the process into steps, so you can anticipate difficulties and challenges ahead.

? HOW TO USE IT

The Building Partnerships Map describes a series of phases which a partnership might involve. The map indicates what is needed in each phase to make such partnerships work, offering guidelines rather than rules. Each phase, as outlined on the worksheet, is important and should not be neglected if the partnership is to remain balanced and on course to achieve its goals.

To work well, partnerships need to be mutually beneficial to the partners involved.

You can use the Building Partnerships Map to analyse at what phase of partnership you and your partner are, so that you can move through the next phases to build a strong partnership together.

- Identify the stage that shows where you are at
- Identify the stage where you would like to be
- Use the template as a map to build a pathway towards that stage

The mapped pathway gives an outline of the activities that need to be done in between.

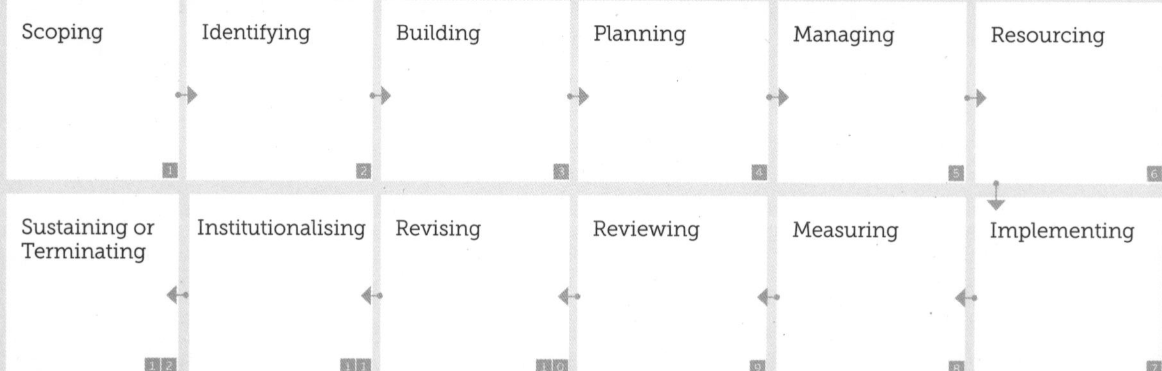

I want to develop a clear plan
for working with other groups that have the same vision as me.

BUILDING PARTNERSHIPS MAP

Scoping
Understanding the challenge; gathering information; consulting with stakeholders and with potential external resource providers; building a vision of / for the partnership

1

Identifying
Identifying potential partners and - if suitable - securing their involvement; motivating them and encouraging them to work together

2

Building
Partners build their working relationship through agreeing with the goals, objectives and core principles that will underpin their partnership

3

Planning
Partners plan programme of activities and begin to outline a coherent project

4

Managing
Partners explore structure and management of their partnership - medium to long-term

5

Resourcing
Partners (and other supporters) identify and mobilise cash and non-cash resources

6

Implementing
Once resources are in place and project details agreed, the implementation process starts - working to a pre-agreed timetable and (ideally) to specific deliverables

7

Measuring
Measuring and reporting on impact and effectiveness - outputs and outcomes. Is the partnership achieving its goals?

8

Reviewing
Reviewing the partnership: what is the impact of the partnership on partner organisations? Is it time for some partners to leave and / or new partners to join?

9

Revising
Revising the partnership, programme(s) or project(s) in the light of experience

10

Institutionalising
Building appropriate structures and mechanisms for the partnership to ensure longer-term commitment and continuity

11

Sustaining or Terminating
Building sustainability or agreeing on an appropriate conclusion

12

Building feedback cycles within interconnected phases of a complex sanitation project.

I want to develop a clear plan by improving upon what I've done before

LEARNING LOOP

INSPIRED BY

IDEO (2011) Deliver: Create a learning plan, p145. In: IDEO, Human Centered Design Toolkit. Edition - 2. London: IDEO.

LEVEL OF INVOLVEMENT

FAIRLY SIMPLE, SELF ADMINISTERED TOOL
needs relatively less time.

What is it & why should I do it?

Learning is an ongoing cyclical process. The **Learning Loop** is a tool that helps you to define how the work you do now informs what you do next. It provides a high-level perspective on how implementing social change can be broken down into a gradual process of iterative cycles.

The worksheet, inspired by the Learning Plan from IDEO (2011), describes four different stages that your work might pass through in a cycle of continual improvement. Using this tool can help understand the different phases involved when trying to implement your ideas. By reflecting on the process involved, it can help you to understand what to do next.

? HOW TO USE IT

This tool offers you a framework to plan with and work in. Each of the four components relate to the methods, systems and processes that your organisation works with. It helps you check whether your organisation actually learns from its experiences (both success and failure) and is improving continuously.

Use the Learning Loop worksheet to make notes in each of the four quadrants. There is no strict start or end to this process - you could use the worksheet to plan a new project or make notes on a current project. Essentially the learnings you gain by collecting stories, feedback or outcomes will help you to reconsider and improve the next steps in your process.

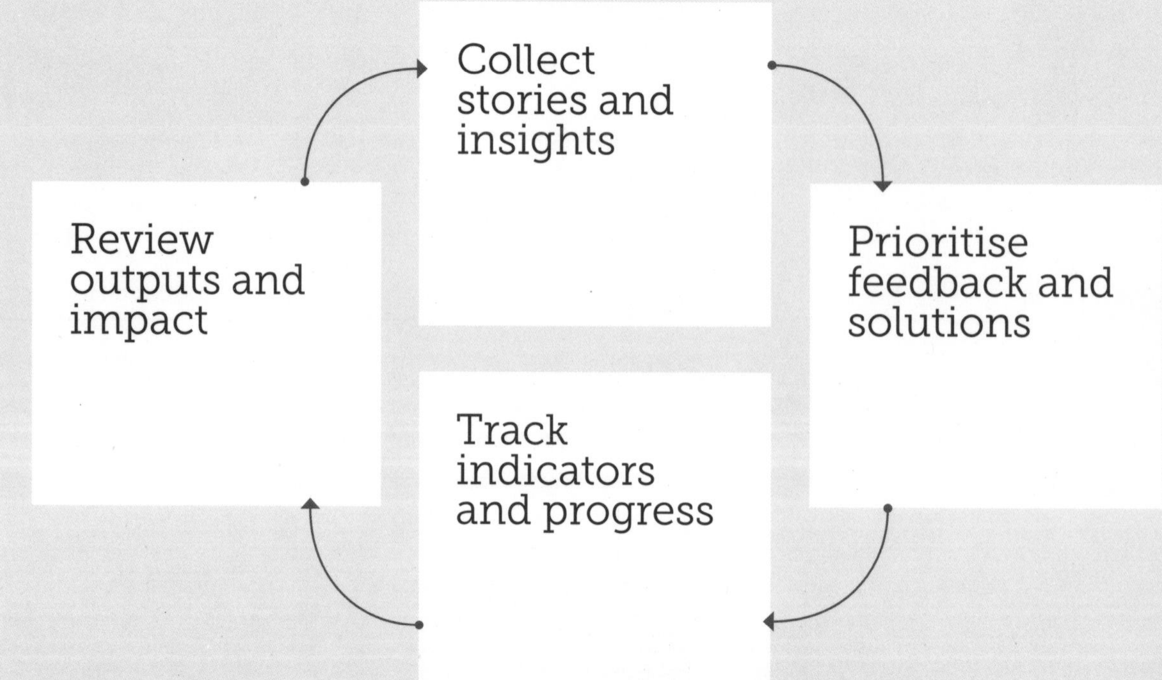

I want to develop a clear plan
by improving upon what I've done before

LEARNING LOOP

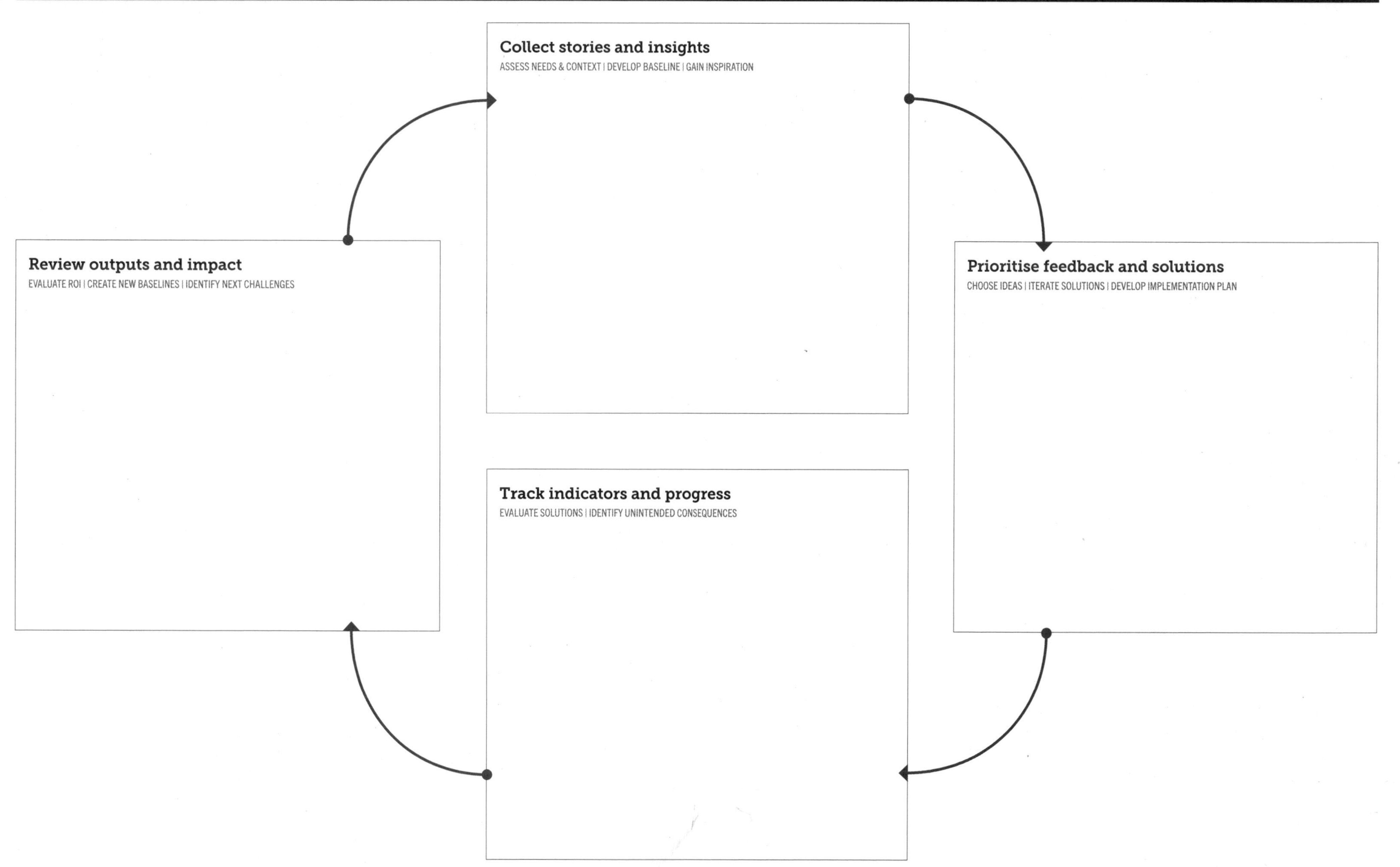

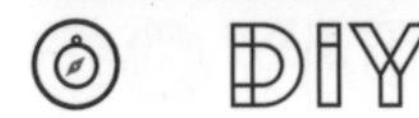

DIY

CASE STUDY

TOOL USED: BUSINESS MODEL CANVAS

ORGANISATION: SBCSOL - INCUBADORA DE EMPREENDIMENTOS SOLIDARIOS

COUNTRY: BRAZIL

SECTOR: ENTREPRENEURSHIP AND SKILL DEVELOPMENT

ROLE: SOCIAL DESIGNER

CONTACT PERSON: RENATA MENDES

EMAIL: RENATACM@UOL.COM.BR

TWO MEMBERS FROM THE 'NÓ CEGO CIA DE PALHAÇOS' COLLECTIVE.

Currently the clowns have very scarce infrastructure (such as space for physical activity, financial support and marketing resources) and while they are extremely skilled and passionate about what they do, they are slightly disheartened by the lack of 'paid work'.

The Nó Cego Cia de Palhaços ('Palhaços' translates to 'clowns' in Portuguese) is a group of four people who believe in the power of clown training as a healing tool for 'a society whose greatest need is 'the experience of love'. They work with the Center for Psychosocial Support (CAPS), where they use the craft of clowning (and other creative psychotherapy techniques) as a restorative instrument for members undergoing mental treatment and marginalised people who are physically or emotionally unstable. Their work relies heavily on skilled group coordinators who are passionate about craft and who desire recognition through social work, but still need to be incentivised through some professional income generation.

RENATA EXPLAINS THE DIFFERENT CATEGORY HEADS IN THE ADAPTED BUSINESS MODEL CANVAS WORKSHEET

THE PALHAÇOS LOOKING AT THEIR COMPLETED CANVAS AND FIGURING OUT NEXT STEPS FOR THEIR RENEWED BUSINESS MODEL

WHY WE USED THE TOOL:

The Nó Cego Cia de Palhaços are being incubated at the SBCSol Programme, where they are currently figuring out ways to broaden their avenues and resources. Though their service is well figured out, the business aspect of the palhaços' work is still in its embryonic stages. We decided to use the Business Model Canvas tool to create a new value proposition for the clowns, one that conveys they are a professional and competitive service while staying true to their rich history and experience. We wanted to make the foundation of this business plan as participatory as possible and included as many people we could to help us build the canvas.

HOW WE USED THE TOOL:

To make it more relevant to the palhaços', we adapted the tool and added more context specific questions to it. Then to help the ideas flow better, we broke the activity into 2 parts :

Initial Brainstorm : We started the activity as a big group, the participants could pick any number of questions they wanted to answer, in any particular order.

Detailing : After this first step, we put together teams of people with similar ideas and asked them to elaborate on each subject, particularly the value proposition. Breaking up into these panels helped the group create detailed content for the canvas.

The tool introduces the concept of 'business thinking' to people who have no prior experience as entrepreneurs.

It helped the palhaços organise their thoughts and was instrumental in helping them construct concrete goals for themselves and detailing out activities needed for each stage.

RESULTS OF USING THE TOOL:

The tool introduces the concept of 'business thinking' to people who have no prior experience as entrepreneurs. It helped the palhaços organise their thoughts and was instrumental in helping them construct concrete goals for themselves and detailing out activities needed for each stage. Furthermore, the tool provided an accessible language for everyone, even those with lower education. Guided by the questions on the canvas, we built a very solid value proposition, which guided the development of other areas of the business model.

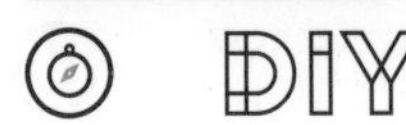 DIY

CASE STUDY

TOOL USED: BUSINESS MODEL CANVAS

ORGANISATION: SBCSOL - INCUBADORA DE EMPREENDIMENTOS SOLIDARIOS

COUNTRY: BRAZIL

SECTOR: ENTREPRENEURSHIP AND SKILL DEVELOPMENT

ROLE: SOCIAL DESIGNER

CONTACT PERSON: RENATA MENDES

EMAIL: RENATACM@UOL.COM.BR

Based near the southern coast of Sao Paulo, the Criqué Caiçara's formed by seven local residents, is part of a traditional community and is supported by the Elos Institute and the NGO Central Artesol.

The aim of this community is to preserve the culture, the environment and generate job opportunities using artisanal know how. From caixeta, the wood that is native to the area, products are created using the elements found in Juréia (one of Brazil's Ecological Stations i.e. preservation area). These include educational toys, accessories and home wares.

(TOP) ARTISANS CREATING CRAFT PRODUCTS IN THE WOOD WORKSHOP; (BOTTOM) THE PARTICIPATORY BUSINESS MODEL CANVAS EXERCISE WITH THE COMMUNITY.

WHY WE USED THE TOOL:

We wanted to build the business on the existing strengths of the work - on what was already being done, and create a social business that is sensitive to the local environment, community and the craft. We wanted to start building the foundation of a business plan with as much participation as possible so that the people who form the community also choose how their business would be.

HOW WE USED THE TOOL:

Until now the group was only looking at activities, but seeing all aspects of a business laid out in one visual, helped us connect the different elements and activities in the business. The key activities thus became the point from which we started filling out our Canvas. This exercise generated a flow chart that contained all areas of the business, and who is responsible for each of the areas.

We wanted to build the business on the existing strengths of the work - on what was already being done, and create a social business that is sensitive to the local environment, community and the craft.

RESULTS OF USING THE TOOL:

Having the business model laid out in a one sheet visual helped the group find connections between the different aspects of business while also coming up with new ideas and even repurposing known information in a new way. The tool enabled discussion of each area of the business, which was especially important for Criqué Caiçara where different functions are performed by the same people due to it being a small group.

Crique Caiçara is a family group which includes both young children and their mothers as part of their group. The Business Model Canvas was key in the active participation of all, helping capture aspirations of both older and younger participants in a short time. The tool is useful to facilitate introducing business concepts for the artisans, helping them acquire a more entrepreneurial outlook by focusing towards more concrete goals.

This workshop helped optimise our work: improving time management, helping better use of skills.

CASE STUDY

TOOL USED: SWOT ANALYSIS

ORGANISATION: SANERGY

COUNTRY: KENYA

SECTOR: WASH (WATER, SANITATION AND HYGIENE)

ROLE: SPECIAL PROJECTS CONSULTANT

CONTACT PERSON: MARIELLE SCHWEICKART

EMAIL: MARIELLE@SANER.GY

"I am working on a project to diversify the income streams of micro-entrepreneurs in the community in which we work. I am actually well into this project and I wasn't attempting to solve a problem, per se, but I thought that some of the tools could help me think through the next few stages of it. I used the SWOT Analysis tool as a self evaluation exercise, but decided to change it a bit, by pretending I had filled it for my project 2 months ago."

> "This tool worked well and helped me view my project as holistically as possible and I think it would have been useful if I used it in the beginning of the project."

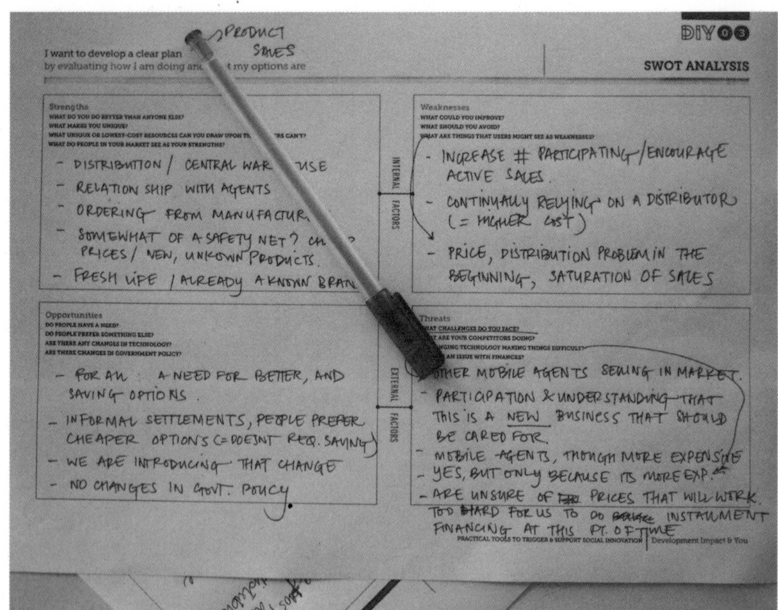

THE FILLED OUT SWOT ANALYSIS SHEET FOR A PRODUCT SALES PROJECT AT SANERGY.

DIY 

CASE STUDY

TOOL USED: BUILDING PARTNERSHIPS MAP

ORGANISATION: FHI360

COUNTRY: INDIA

SECTOR: PUBLIC HEALTH, NUTRITION AND WASH

ROLE: TEAM LEADER

CONTACT PERSON: SUBBANAICKER KRISHNASWAMY

EMAIL: SKRISHNASWAMY@MPTAST.ORG

THE VARIOUS DIMENSIONS OF BUILDING PARTNERSHIPS FOR MPTAST PROGRAMMES.

MPTAST (Madhya Pradesh Technical Assistance and Support Team) is a part of the MP Health Sector Reforms Project (MPHSRP) and supports the State Health department in achieving milestones for improved health, nutrition, water, sanitation and hygiene services in 16 identified, underserved districts in the state of Madhya Pradesh, India.

The project anticipates that by 2015, Madhya Pradesh families and communities will benefit from an integrated package of high-impact and high-quality health services delivered in a coordinated, sustainable and cost-effective manner and requires partnering with several stakeholders (operating at a micro and macro scale) to help achieve this impact.

We are currently in the process of identifying various partners that will work in 8 districts (serving a population of roughly 72 million people) on various aspects of the programme :

- NGO Partners who are meant to carry out programme evaluations in the form of baseline and mid term research and an impact assessment at the end of the project.
- Capacity building NGOs who develop and modify Participatory Learning Action (PLA*) modules and are also responsible for putting a management information system in place.
- An implementing partner for rolling out the PLA modules.
- An agency to provide technical support to government counterparts, i.e. the State Livelihood Mission (SRLM), and help them identify a HR agency to recruit and manage the HR on behalf of the government.

*Participatory Learning and Action (PLA) is a form of action research. It is a practical, adaptive research strategy that enables diverse groups and individuals to learn, work and act together in a co-operative manner, to focus on issues of joint concern, identify challenges and generate positive responses in a collaborative and democratic manner.

WHY WE USED THE TOOL:

Bringing these partners with varying levels and varying nature of involvement has proven to be a real challenge for us. We used the Building Partnerships tool to map out how to proceed with engaging with these four specific stakeholders, even before they have been identified.

RESULTS OF USING THE TOOL:

This tool analytically separated several related concepts/dimensions to forging partnerships which needs to be kept in mind while building them. It becomes very important to recognise these finer points so that none are missed out however small it may be.

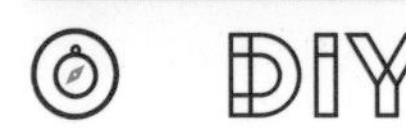

CASE STUDY

TOOL USED: LEARNING LOOP

ORGANISATION: FHI360

COUNTRY: INDIA

SECTOR: PUBLIC HEALTH, NUTRITION AND WATER, SANITATION & HYGIENE (WASH)

ROLE: TEAM LEADER

CONTACT PERSON: SUBBANAICKER KRISHNASWAMY

EMAIL: SKRISHNASWAMY@MPTAST.ORG

The problem I was trying to tackle is that of under reporting/non-reporting of maternal and child deaths, which are crucial social indicators of Public Health & Nutrition.

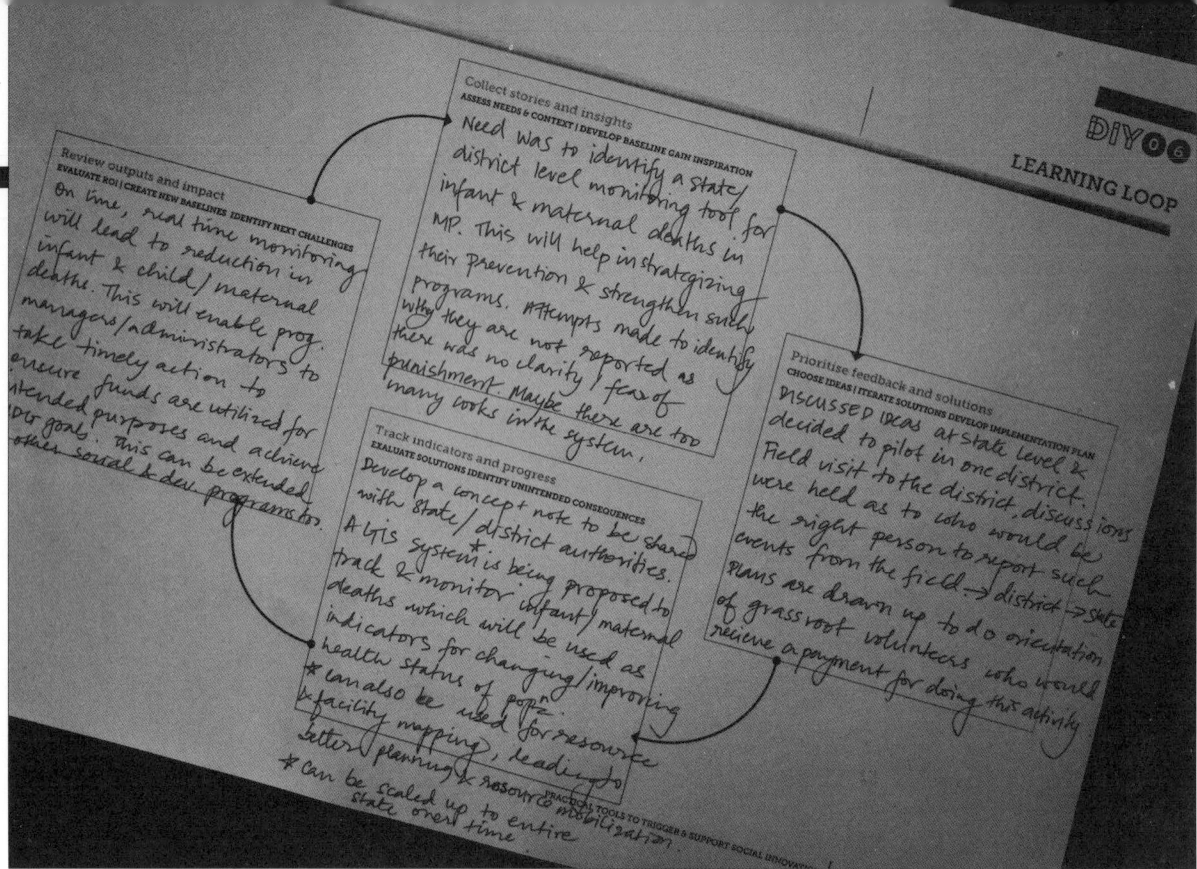

A LEARNING LOOP PLAN FOR THE STATE INFANT AND MOTHER HEALTH AND NUTRITION PROGRAMME MANAGED BY MPTAST.

I head the MPTAST that gives technical assistance and management support to Government of Madhya Pradesh, a central Indian State, covering the areas of Health and Family Welfare, Women Child Development and Panchayati Raj and Rural Development.

This under reporting/ non-reporting leads to an even bigger problem of hampering corrective measures that could actually help reduce the numbers of maternal and child deaths.

WHY & HOW WE USED THE TOOL:

I used the Learning Loop with the participation of all the stake holders involved in finding a solution. The Monitoring and Evaluation (M&E) specialist along with my service delivery personnel visited one of the pilot districts to find out the possible channels for reporting the deaths of mothers and children more quickly. This was discussed with various stakeholders - grassroots health care workers, village level volunteers and the village level nutrition workers to establish their awareness levels and the reasons for not reporting these cases.

RESULTS OF USING THE TOOL:

We then worked with the MCTS (Mother & Child Tracking System), which is an online monitoring software, developed by Government of India with an objective to track the different services being provided/ to be provided to a pregnant mother right from conception until the baby is a year old. The problem and our learnings from the pilot district was then discussed with the District health authorities who agreed to try out a new system. The new system was also proposed to the state leadership, who readily agreed to it for monitoring maternal and child deaths.

This is a good tool that spells out the inter-relatedness of a social phenomenon and how to address them in a very succinct manner.

One can use it literally for any social indicator that requires an innovative solution.

This would help in understanding the intra and inter district differentials and the factors that possibly contribute to this phenomenon and alert the authorities for taking timely action. This is a good tool that spells out the inter relatedness of a social phenomenon and how to address them in a very succinct manner. One can use it literally for any social indicator that requires a innovative solution.

We will be rolling out the concept very soon and are in the process of refining the concept for buy-in from the State government, based on the pilot results from one district.

Experience research on household water collection issues in the urban 'kampungs' in South-east Asia.

I want to clarify my priorities by learning from first hand experiences

EXPERIENCE TOUR

INSPIRED BY
Design Council (2011) Service Safari. In: Keeping Connected Design Challenge.

LEVEL OF INVOLVEMENT

MORE COMPLEX TOOL that should ideally be done over a few days. Given the strategic nature of the inputs/outputs, this needs consultations with seniors, peers and ideally needs to be revised after a first pass.

EXPERIENCE TOUR

What is it & why should I do it?

Going on an **Experience Tour** means immersing yourself totally in a particular environment so you can gain a first-hand perspective of the situation or context. Experience Tours can help 'ground' your thinking; they give you a clear perspective for developing ideas that are intimately connected with the people you're working for.

This tool provides a structure for reflecting upon and collecting insights from your first hand experiences. There are guidelines to help you focus on the experiences of the people you are trying to understand, and to collect the type of materials you will need afterwards to start developing ideas.

? HOW TO USE IT

Experience Tours are a good way to spark inspirations by learning first-hand about what makes a great experience - or even what not to do, in the event that you encounter a negative experience. As going on an Experience Tour often means being out and about, it may be difficult to make structured notes on a worksheet. Take a good look at the questions on the worksheet before you go out to get some prompts on the things to look out for.

You can either fill out the worksheet as the Experience Tour progresses, or use it to jot down quick reminders and then sit down later to fill in all the details.

The idea is to really try and reflect upon the experience and understand the deeper layers - think about how it made you feel, as well as exactly what happened. You can complete one worksheet for every tour you make and later compare these to find relevant connections or even differences.

The questions on the worksheet are examples, you can customise the worksheet to make it relevant to your work.

What is the focus for this tour?

What are the practices observed?

Who is involved?

What information is used?
What's missing?

What products are used?

What is the environment like?

What works well?

What doesn't work well?
What can be improved?

Additional notes & remarks

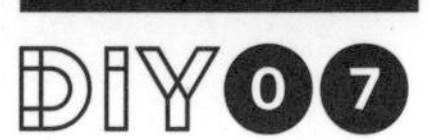

I want to clarify my priorities
by learning from first hand experiences

EXPERIENCE TOUR

What is the focus for this tour?

What are the practices observed?

Who is involved?

What information is used?
What's missing?

What products are used?

What is the environment like?

What works well?

What doesn't work well?
What can be improved?

Additional notes & remarks

Reframing work process challenges faced by development practitioners.

I want to clarify my priorities by focusing on key critical issues

PROBLEM DEFINITION

INSPIRED BY
Julier J., Kimbell L. (2012) Problem Definition. p30. In: The Social Design Methods Menu.

LEVEL OF INVOLVEMENT

FAIRLY SIMPLE, SELF ADMINISTERED TOOL
needs relatively less time.

What is it & why should I do it?

Defining a problem is a deceptively simple task - what at first seems to be the problem is often merely a symptom of a deeper problem. This tool works to both open a problem up - presenting it in a way that can be examined from a number of angles - as well as helping to define the wider context and associated issues involved.

This is particularly effective when trying to focus a team of people on the key problems at hand. This tool has been designed to structure the analysis of a particular problem in a way that makes good use of your time. It introduces a small set of key criteria by which an issue can be articulated and assessed, which makes the activity highly efficient. It also gives you a standardised way to compare several different problems which might seem to be very different on the surface.

HOW TO USE IT

Go through the Problem Definition worksheet individually or in small teams and reflect on a specific issue you have identified, exchanging thoughts while writing down your notes. The key aim here is to capture, compare and discuss different viewpoints on the problem. You can then review the notes and discuss with your team members whether you are making the same assumptions, and whether you are framing things in the same way.

This exercise may lead you to 'reframe' the problem you initially addressed – for example, what happens if you see older people as having capacities, rather than needs? Reframing problems in such a way can offer clues to how the solution can take shape.

Working on a Problem Definition worksheet with not only your team members, but together with other stakeholders, will usually bring up new contexts. For instance, working with service users, staff or volunteers may provide a slightly different angle to the tool than when working with managers or entrepreneurs. Feel free to experiment and rephrase questions in the worksheet to keep them relevant in such situations.

What is the key issue you are trying to address and why is it important?

Who is it a problem for?

What social/cultural factors shape this problem?

What evidence do you have that this is worth the investment?

Can you think of this problem in a different way? Can you reframe it?

I want to clarify my priorities
by focusing on key critical issues

PROBLEM DEFINITION

What is the key issue you are trying to address and why is it important?	Who is it a problem for?	What social/cultural factors shape this problem?	What evidence do you have that this is worth the investment?	Can you think of this problem in a different way? Can you reframe it?

Understanding user experience aspects of training modules around employability for out-of-school youth.

I want to clarify my priorities by breaking down a complex issue

▽

CAUSES DIAGRAM

INSPIRED BY
Namahn and Yellow Window Service Design, Design Flanders (2012) Cause Diagram. In: Service design toolkit.

LEVEL OF INVOLVEMENT

FAIRLY SIMPLE, SELF ADMINISTERED TOOL
needs relatively less time.

CAUSES DIAGRAM

What is it & why should I do it?

What is the root cause of a problem? Often there isn't one simple answer. The bigger the problem, the more likely it is that the roots will be widespread, and mapping out the causes can quickly get out of hand, making the task seem overwhelming.

The **Causes Diagram** helps you think of a problem in a thorough manner and provides a structured way to analyse it. It pushes you to deconstruct all possible causes for the problem rather than the obvious ones. You can use it both to analyse a new problem and to highlight the gaps in an existing one.

It differentiates causes from effects or symptoms, giving you a better idea of the solutions needed to solve a problem permanently, and helps to build a shared understanding of what it is you're working on.

HOW TO USE IT

First, identify and write down the core problem you are trying to resolve.

Working your way from this starting point, write down the direct, underlying and contributing symptoms you see as a result of it. These may be people involved with the problem, systems, equipment, materials, external forces, etc. Try drawing out as many contributing factors as possible.

Now fill out the causes that correspond to these symptoms. Once the worksheet has been filled out, go through each symptom and cause with your team and consider if they are correctly placed, and discuss what you can learn from this in terms of clarifying your aims.

Be careful to not mix the causes of a problem with its symptoms as you note these down - a cause is the reason why something happens, while a symptom is usually what we see as the end result of the problem.

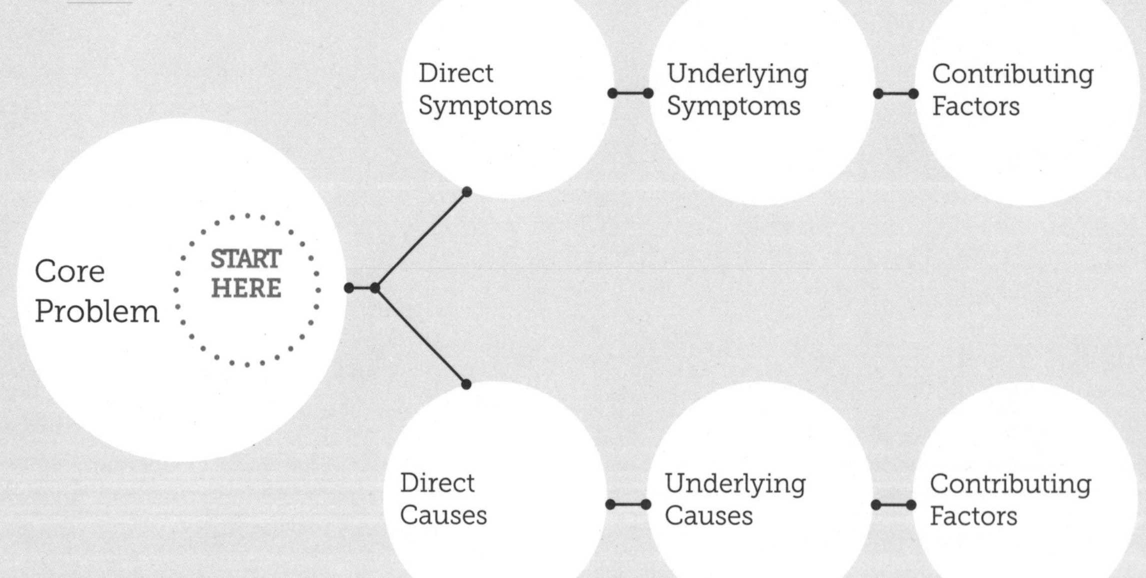

I want to clarify my priorities
by breaking down a complex issue

CAUSES DIAGRAM

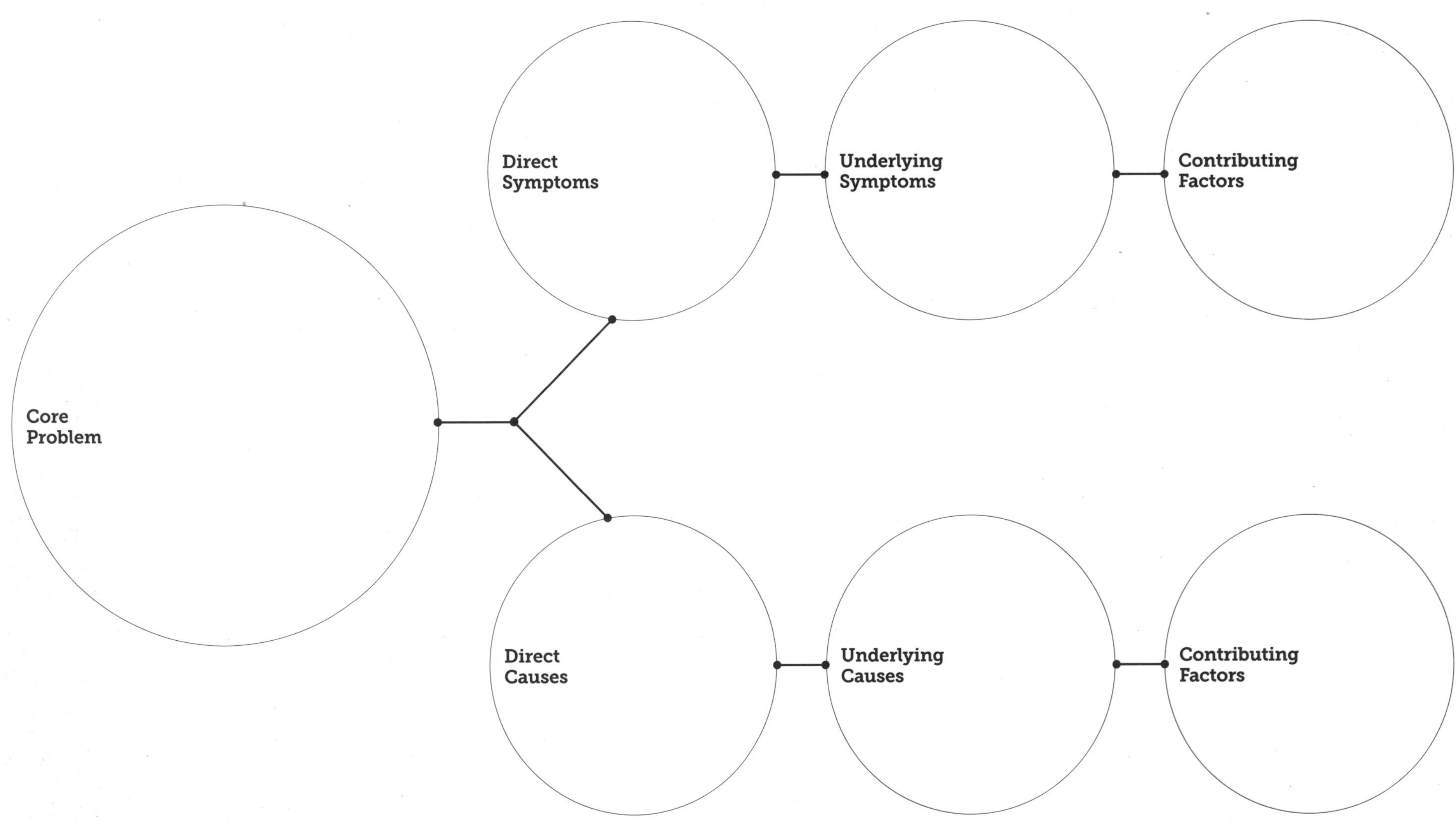

Using the Theory of Change in a Workshop helping social entrepreneurs connect the outcomes of their work to its wider impact

Theory of Change

WHAT IS THE PROBLEM YOU ARE TRYING TO SOLVE ?

WHO IS YOUR KEY AUDIENCE?

WHAT IS YOUR ENTRY POINT TO REACH YOUR AUDIENCE ?

HUB Launchpad and Futuregov at Outcome Fest, London 2014

I want to clarify my priorities by defining my goals and the path to reach them

▽

THEORY OF CHANGE

INSPIRED BY
Nesta (2011) Theory of Change.

LEVEL OF INVOLVEMENT

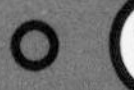  

REQUIRES SOME DIALOGUE with colleagues/ peers. plan for some time to interact and fill out in collaboration over a day maybe.

What is it & why should I do it?

Setting up a **Theory of Change** is like making a road map that outlines the steps by which you plan to achieve your goal. It helps you define whether your work is contributing towards achieving the impact you envision, and if there is another way that you need to consider as well.

The Theory of Change tool not only helps to clearly articulate and connect your work to your bigger goal, it also allows you to spot potential risks in your plan by sharing the underlying assumptions in each step. In large organisations, when there may be several projects running simultaneously, the Theory of Change helps to map these different projects first and then consider how they link and relate to each other.

This tool can also aid in aligning team members to the larger end goal, and help them understand their role in achieving it.

HOW TO USE IT

Start by noting down the main problem you want to solve, and also your long term vision on the change you want to accomplish. Then complete the other boxes, such as your key audience and your entry point to reach that audience. Try to be as specific as possible because it will help you to come up with more effective actions that you can take.

Work outwards from your defining problem, and towards your long-term impact. Write down the people that are most affected by the issue that you've identified and who you hope to help with your work – this could be a small community group or a large organisation. Then think about where to start your work, you may need to find a place, a person or a thing that will be your first port of call. Try to think of some practical steps that you can take to make changes – like creating partnerships, or making tweaks to existing processes. Try to keep these as action-oriented as possible.

And finally, what would the immediate results or outcomes be? These could be tangible results that you can show to other people to clarify how your work is making a difference. List the key outcomes that your activity would lead to: these are the preconditions that you need to realise your vision.

As you fill each of the boxes in the worksheet, it is critical to also reflect on the key assumptions that underpin these steps in your work. This may help you to spot potential risks or connections between the different projects.

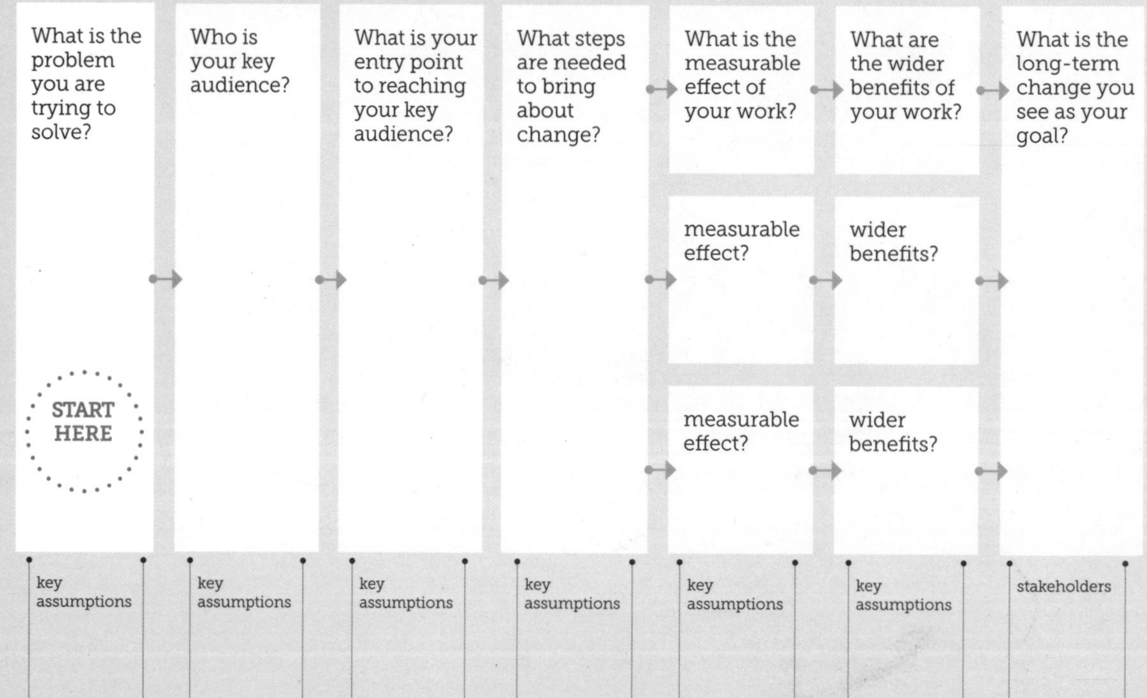

I want to clarify my priorities
by defining my goals and the path to reach them

THEORY OF CHANGE

What is the problem you are trying to solve?

Who is your key audience?

What is your entry point to reaching your audience?

What steps are needed to bring about change?

What is the measurable effect of your work?

What are the wider benefits of your work?

Measurable effect?

Wider benefits?

Measurable effect?

Wider benefits?

What is the long-term change you see as your goal?

KEY ASSUMPTIONS

KEY ASSUMPTIONS

KEY ASSUMPTIONS

KEY ASSUMPTIONS

KEY ASSUMPTIONS

KEY ASSUMPTIONS

STAKEHOLDERS

DIY

CASE STUDY

TOOL USED: PROBLEM DEFINITION, CAUSES DIAGRAM

ORGANISATION: UNDP UZBEKISTAN

COUNTRY: UZBEKISTAN

SECTOR: COMMUNITY OUTREACH / EDUCATION

ROLE: COMMUNITY OUTREACH SPECIALIST

CONTACT PERSON: ANDREAS KARPATI

EMAIL: ANDREAS.KARPATI@UNDP.ORG

Development Fund of Children's Sport under the Ministry of Public Education in Uzbekistan was concerned that despite a large-scale investment programme into sports complexes, the use of these facilities has been below expectations, especially outside Tashkent.

WORKSHOPS WITH STUDENTS TO IDENTIFY PROBLEMS AND RELEVANT CAUSES FOR UNDER-PARTICIPATION OF SCHOOL STUDENTS IN LOCAL SPORTS PROGRAMMES.

The Children's Sports Fund is particularly concerned about the participation of girls from rural areas in sports, who often miss out on the benefits of doing sports due to a lack of parental awareness, encouragement or even permission. Despite major investments into infrastructure and programmes guaranteeing free access to sports facilities, how do we get people to use the facilities?

WHY WE USED THE TOOL:

We organised a workshop on social innovation with young citizens - students from a local partner university, focused on the 'sport for social inclusion'. Promising project proposals that come out of this, were eligible to be considered for a small grant award of up to $1,500. While making these project proposals, we used a number of tools such as Target Group, Personas to think about the users and Problem Definition, Causes Diagram to think about possible problems and solutions.

The tools were chosen along three main criteria:

1. Suitability for a small-scale volunteer project without commercial elements.
2. Applicable for an early, pre-prototyping stage of the social innovation process (emphasis on ideation, problem definition, working out users).
3. Can be carried out in less than an hour in a classroom/workshop setting.

Using the tools helped to familiarise ourselves with the problem and root out actionable causes, some of which were unexpected and new to us.

HOW WE USED THE TOOL:

We used Problem Definition and Causes Diagram in a workshop to help encourage students think more broadly about the problem, and possible solutions. However, it was only after encouraging students to ask successive 'why' questions that the exercise really led to new insights. Often they would jump ahead without identifying more nuances and identify 'economic problems' or 'traditions' as second-order causes. Once encouraged to be more specific however, they found interesting and sometimes unexpected causes for low participation in sports, including for example the fear of injuries (in conjunction with low standards of health services) or lack of street lighting (in conjunction with safety concerns).

RESULTS OF USING THE TOOL:

The Problem Definition tool aids to define and to realise a certain problem more deeply, and the Causes Diagram helps collect all factors and causes of that problem, so one is able to tackle it. Using the tools helped to familiarise ourselves with the problem and root out actionable causes, some of which were unexpected and new to us.

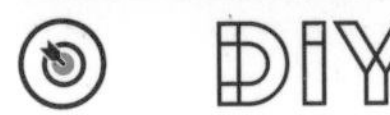

CASE STUDY

TOOL USED: THEORY OF CHANGE, CAUSES DIAGRAM

ORGANISATION: MP TECHNICAL ASSISTANCE AND SUPPORTIVE TEAM (MPTAST)

COUNTRY: INDIA

SECTOR: PUBLIC HEALTH, NUTRITION AND WATER, SANITATION & HYGIENE (WASH)

ROLE: DISTRICT PROJECT COORDINATOR

CONTACT PERSON: RAVI KOMMURI

EMAIL: RKOMMURI@MPTAST.ORG

USING THE THEORY OF CHANGE AND CAUSES DIAGRAM TOOL WITH THE AUXILIARY NURSE MIDWIFE, BLOCK PROJECT MANAGER AND MULTI PURPOSE WORKER IN THE VILLAGE.

FINAL THEORY OF CHANGE WORKSHEET THAT CULMINATED FROM THE GROUP EXERCISE.

I have been working with fhi360 in assisting the Government of Madhya Pradesh (MP) to implement MPHSRP (Madhya Pradesh Health Sector Reforms Programme) since a year.

MCTS (Mother & Child Tracking System) is an online monitoring software which has been developed by Government of India with an objective to track the different services being provided/ to be provided to a pregnant mother right from conception until the baby turns one year old.

Madhya Pradesh, a state in central India has very high infant and mother mortality rates, compared to the national average. Our programme helps strengthen the system and we work closely with the Health Department, WCD (Women & Child Development) & PHED (Public Health Engineering Department) departments aiming to reduce MMR (Maternal Mortality Ratio), IMR (Infant Mortality Ratio), Malnutrition & TFR (Total Fertility Rate) in the state of Madhya Pradesh in India.

The tracking system still needs to be worked upon further before it can be implemented.

WHY WE USED THE TOOL:

My team mates and I used the Theory of Change and Causes Diagram in one combination and SWOT Analysis, Question Ladder and the Critical Task list in another combination. Our aim was to find ways to strengthen the usage of the MCTS software and also re-define roles, incentives and contingency strategies for all the people and stakeholders responsible for its functioning. We did this by first using a set of tools to re-visit and resolve the problem at hand, and then using another set of tools to identify potential team members and a critical pathway to implement our solution.

HOW WE USED THE TOOL:

We tested these tools as a pilot in one of the villages in Jabalpur district, Madhya Pradesh. First, I explained the purpose of doing the whole exercise to my team and with their help tried to get an idea of :

- exactly what is going on?
- who are the people involved and what their roles are?
- what are the bottlenecks that we should work towards to solve the issue?

We then used a combination of Theory of Change and Causes Diagram.

THEORY OF CHANGE

To give a clear idea on what is planned for change – i.e. updating the service in the MCTS system and how it affects their everyday work, how it will help the Programme Manager for decision making and how it is going to impact the overall Infant Mortality Rate over a period of time.

CAUSES DIAGRAM

Identify the bottlenecks which are hindering the MCTS service from updating. To learn from all the root issues and devise a better solution accordingly.

RESULTS OF USING THE TOOL:

The Theory of Change tool helped the team understand that even their role as grassroot workers can contribute to a larger change over time. This was key to achieve any success for the programme and helping create an attitude change towards their work. The tool also helped iron out inefficiencies in the current system in a holistic manner.

The Causes Diagram helped the team realise that while there exists a messy array of convoluted issues, distilling it to the one or two more important and actionable problems was a better strategy. This tool helped the team understand and define the cause of current inefficiencies in a structured manner and helped them identify what to work towards to fix a core problem.

CASE STUDY

TOOL USED: CAUSES DIAGRAM

ORGANISATION: SANERGY

COUNTRY: KENYA

SECTOR: WATER, SANITATION & HYGIENE (WASH)

CONTACT PERSON: SIMON DIXON

EMAIL: SIMON@SANER.GY

We have been having problems boosting individual performances within the Sales and Operations team in our organisation.

Realising that these are often linked to the larger system, we decided to look at the whole Sales and Operations element of the business and form a coordinated change programme.

We have been holding a series of workshops to do this and I thought the Causes Diagram may help us identify issues, understand them and their causes, and subsequently search for solutions.

We adapted the tool to suit our way of presentation and with the outputs we have moved forward to the planning stage wherein we now begin to address the core issues informed by the causes.

I want to collect input from others by observing and learning from everyday life

PEOPLE SHADOWING

INSPIRED BY
Lovlie L.,Reason B.,Polaine A. (2013) Service Design: From Insight to Implementation. p54-p57. Rosenfeld Media

LEVEL OF INVOLVEMENT

REQUIRES SOME DIALOGUE with colleagues/ peers. Plan for some time to interact and fill out in collaboration over a day maybe.

1 1 DIY

PEOPLE SHADOWING

What is it & why should I do it?

Shadowing means just that - becoming someone's shadow for a while. Following someone, or a group of people, as they live their everyday life, or go about their daily work helps to understand the environment they are a part of. It also allows you to observe for yourself the contextual details that can influence a person's behaviour and motivations.

Often doing some Shadowing at the start of a project helps to familiarise yourself with a certain practice or group of people. People's everyday life can be so habitual that some issues may not be as apparent to them - sometimes observing them can reveal hidden aspects that might be the core issue or even possible solution. These observations can act not only as inspiration but also a guide to help reach the core of how your work impacts people.

? HOW TO USE IT

Shadowing involves making many choices - not just who to follow, but also when and how to be actively involved when you get there. You also need to think about the kind of things you're looking out for, and the ways in which you might want to record what you find. The key is preparation - balancing the need to structure what you find while staying open to the unexpected. This tool includes a quick checklist and a format to note down these findings.

This worksheet indicates some of the things you might want to record when shadowing. Don't be afraid to experiment - whether you're silently observing or actively involved will very much depend on each situation you're in. Fill out the worksheet for each person you follow. Ask your team to fill out a similar sheet for each person they follow. This is a structured way to compare your observations across the various 'participants' you and your team shadowed.

The observations you find relevant depend on the focus of your project. These could be about the people they meet, places they go to, or how they organise their life. Feel free to customise the boxes on the worksheet - the ones here are examples to trigger some ideas.

It might be a good idea to ask a person's permission in case you want to follow them closely, though it is also possible to observe your participant from a distance. This may depend on what is socially accepted within the specific situation or culture. Please do respect the person's space and make sure they are comfortable. You don't want to break the natural flow of how they go about their everyday life.

Where & When

Who

Key findings

Likes	Dislikes	Habits
Activities	**Objects**	**Space**

I want to collect input from others
by defining my goals and the path to reach them

PEOPLE SHADOWING

Where & When

LOCATION:
DATE:
TIME:

Who

PERSON SHADOWED:
AGE:
GENDER:
REASON FOR SHADOWING:

Key findings

Likes

eg.: observations on personal preferences

Dislikes

eg.: observations on particular concerns

Habits

eg.: observations on existing routines

Activities

eg.: observations on actions triggered by situation

Objects

eg.: observations on the use of specific objects

Space

eg.: observations on the effect of the environment

Understanding sanitation behaviours and perceptions in urban slums in India.

I want to collect input from others in a conversation that uncovers their perspective

INTERVIEW GUIDE

INSPIRED BY
IDEO (2012) Develop an interview approach p58. In: Human Centred Design Toolkit.

LEVEL OF INVOLVEMENT

REQUIRES SOME DIALOGUE with colleagues/ peers. Plan for some time to interact and fill out in collaboration over a day maybe.

INTERVIEW GUIDE

What is it & why should I do it?

The easiest way to understand a person is to speak to them. Interviews are a way to connect with people; an opportunity to hear them describe their experiences in their own words. Speaking to people about their everyday lives can help you define and describe the problems they face, understand the environment they're part of, and even picture the ways in which you can reach them. Interviews can also act as evidence for why your work is needed or what impact your work is creating.

Getting what you want from an interview however can be harder than you think - what people say and what they actually do are often very different things. Establishing an in-depth understanding of a particular experience might take some time, and requires a series of questions and activities as part of a conversation. Even a short interview can provide a huge amount of information, with masses of material quickly piling up when you start speaking with several people. The **Interview Guide** acts like a checklist to help you prepare a game-plan for an interview.

? HOW TO USE IT

This worksheet is an example of how you can prepare your interview. Depending on the focus of the project, this can also contain other items.

There is usually a mix of practices as well as underlying motivations you want to explore. Focus your questions on asking 'What' and 'How' and then probe deeper into people's motivations by asking 'Why'.

You could follow this three step framework to structure your interview:

Open Up: Make the participant feel at ease with 'warm-up' questions they are comfortable with. (for e.g. Household demographics; Who does what in the household? Some recent anecdotes related to the topic.)

Go Broad: Prompt bigger, wider thinking on related issues that they may not normally address on a daily basis. (Aspirations for the future, How are things connected?)

Probe Deep: Dig deeper on the challenge at hand and prompt with challenging 'what if' scenarios.

There are various ways to elicit and document information during an interview. Make sure to prompt participants to be specific in clarifying their preferences and motivations. You may ask people to simply tell you, but you could also invite them to show things, or maybe make a drawing of particular practices they have (e.g. where is your favourite spot in the room? What is your favourite object in the house?)

Before you do the actual interview, it is wise to practice with your team to get a sense of how to frame the questions for better response. Also think about how you would use these interviews later. This is especially useful if several people will be conducting the interviews.

Show me

Draw it

Think aloud

Be specific

I want to collect input from others
in a conversation that uncovers their perspective

INTERVIEW GUIDE

Show me
If you are in the interviewee's environment, ask him or her to show you the things they interact with (objects, spaces, tools, etc). Capture pictures and notes to jog your memory later. Or, have them walk you through the process.

Draw it
Ask participants to map out their activities and experiences through sketches and diagrams. This is a good way to debunk assumptions and reveal how people perceive and order their activities.

Think aloud
As they perform a process or task, ask participants to describe aloud what they are thinking. This helps uncover their motivations, concerns, perceptions and reasoning.

Be specific
People often generalise about what's typical and leave out rich important details. Instead, ask people to talk about a specific period of time. Instead of what's your typical day like, ask them what happened yesterday.

Investigating household water practices with homemakers in rural India.

I want to collect input from others by getting to the heart of what motivates people

▽

QUESTION LADDER

INSPIRED BY
Project Innovation (2012) Question. In: Social Innovation Toolkit.

LEVEL OF INVOLVEMENT

FAIRLY SIMPLE, SELF ADMINISTERED TOOL
needs relatively less time.

QUESTION LADDER

What is it & why should I do it?

How do you know the right question to ask? Sometimes reaching the right answer means thinking more about the kind of questions you're asking. It might sound simple, but focusing on what you're asking someone is essential for reaching a deeper understanding. The **Question Ladder** is an interview technique that helps you to hone in on a certain topic by asking a series of questions about different aspects related to that topic.

This tool is a quick and easy way to start asking your questions in a few different ways, and to start combining questions in order to reach more complex answers. It provides a structured overview of what goes into a question; it shows how to combine a range of who, what, where, when, why and how questions coupled with the words like is, did, can, will, would and might. This makes it much easier to think about the best way to get to the heart of the issue at hand, and to build chains of questions that will allow you to gradually reach the heart of more complex issues.

HOW TO USE IT

While making a questionnaire or before going for an interview, this worksheet can be used as a series of possible questions from which a final set can be chosen. Use this to practice approaching and exploring an issue through various directions.

Once you have gained some experience with using this technique, you might find yourself automatically using it in conversations or interviews you conduct with people.

simple questions ◄——► complex questions

	Is	Did	Can	Will	Would	Might
Who	Who is	Who did	Who can	Who will	Who would	Who might
What	What is	What did	What can	What will	What would	What might
Where	Where is	Where did	Where can	Where will	Where would	Where might
When	When is	When did	When can	When will	When would	When might
Why	Why is	Why did	Why can	Why will	Why would	Why might
How	How is	How did	How can	How will	How would	How might

I want to collect input from others
by getting to the heart of what motivates people

QUESTION LADDER

SIMPLE QUESTIONS ↔ COMPLEX QUESTIONS

	Is	Did	Can	Will	Would	Might
Who	Who is	Who did	Who can	Who will	Who would	Who might
What	What is	What did	What can	What will	What would	What might
Where	Where is	Where did	Where can	Where will	Where would	Where might
When	When is	When did	When can	When will	When would	When might
Why	Why is	Why did	Why can	Why will	Why would	Why might
How	How is	How did	How can	How will	How would	How might

Creating stories around safe water practices and rituals with schoolchildren.

I want to collect input from others to ensure my work is relevant to the people I'm working for

STORYWORLD

INSPIRED BY
Julier J., Kimbell L. (2012) Storyworld. p24. In: The Social Design Methods Menu.

LEVEL OF INVOLVEMENT

MORE COMPLEX TOOL that should ideally be done over a few days. Given the strategic nature of the inputs/outputs, this needs consultations with seniors, peers and ideally needs to be revised after a first pass.

STORYWORLD

What is it & why should I do it?

Qualitative data collected through interviews and observations can be incredibly rich. A structured way of documenting this for analysis and communication is very important. The **Storyworld** tool provides a useful way to highlight the most relevant insights from your research. It helps you do this without being overwhelmed with details, showing you how to structure your documentation so that the discussions you have afterwards are in tune with the learning requirements.

The tool enables you to bring part of a person's world with you once you start designing a solution that is addressed to them. It allows you to create stories that make people easier to relate to - often closely matching the colour and complexity of somebody's everyday life. These stories can be key triggers to inspire creative ideas.

HOW TO USE IT

You can use Storyworld as an input for a creative workshop. Fill out the worksheet in advance, to provide a structured profile that is relevant to the topic. This offers a useful starting point for a brainstorm on ideas for new solutions.

You can also use Storyworld as a workshop activity by filling out the sections of the worksheet together with your team, while going through selected data from your research. This enables the team to develop a joint understanding of a person and his/her world.

In some situations you can even use Storyworld as a research tool by taking the worksheet to an interview with someone. Together map out the different aspects of themselves and their life as part of your conversation. This works particularly well with active and creative research participants.

Profile	Context		Memorable quotes / Notes on things that stood out
	Connections and Relations	Objects and Places	
	Self		
	Perceptions	Aspirations	

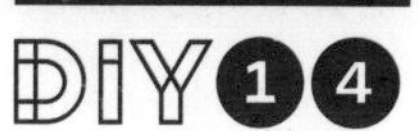

I want to collect input from others
to ensure my work is relevant to the people I'm working for

STORYWORLD

Profile
Add a picture or drawing that represents the person

NAME

AGE

GENDER

FAMILY

LIVING CONTEXT

WORK

PLAY

Context

Connections and Relations
Who is this person connected to? How?
(Include people and organisations)

Objects and Places
What physical and digital objects is this person connected to?
How, where and when?

Self

Perceptions
What does this person think or believe about themselves and the world around them?

Aspirations
How does this person think about their involvement in change?
What shapes this?

Memorable quotes

Notes on things that stood out

CASE STUDY

TOOL USED: INTERVIEW GUIDE, QUESTION LADDER

ORGANISATION: iDE

COUNTRY: CAMBODIA

SECTOR: RURAL POVERTY REDUCTION

ROLE: INNOVATION LEAD

CONTACT PERSON: YI WEI

EMAIL: YWEI@IDE-CAMBODIA.ORG

We were devising an interview guideline to collect information on a certain group of government officials and whether they should be the recommended channel for implementing a social marketing campaign.

We needed to get honest feedback from them and those around them about how appropriate they were to serve this role.

WHY WE USED THE TOOL:

We used the Interview Guide and the Question Ladder tool in tandem to help us take stock - making sure we got all the possible questions out there first, then organising them according to the purpose of the question, and then finally by level of complexity.

HOW WE USED THE TOOL:

We used the tool as a guide to help organise our questions. The most helpful aspect was probably how the tool organised the questions according to complexity. In the Cambodian context, asking a question will most likely not get you the answer right away. Rather, you have to ask the same question in several different ways, and understanding which questions are most complex helped to remind us to ask questions as simply as possible first.

RESULTS OF USING THE TOOL:

We were able to ask questions as directly as possible without getting too complex in the beginning with more abstract ideas such as conditionals.

CONDUCTING A SURVEY WITHIN OUR VIDEO MANAGEMENT AND SOFTWARE TEAM WITH THE QUESTION LADDER TOOL.

DIY

CASE STUDY

TOOL USED: QUESTION LADDER

ORGANISATION: DIGITAL GREEN

COUNTRY: INDIA

SECTOR: ICT IN AGRICULTURE

ROLE: ASSISTANT SOFTWARE ENGINEER

CONTACT PERSON: NIKITA DAGAR

EMAIL: NIKITA@DIGITALGREEN.ORG

Digital green uses ICT to curate and share best practices (in the form of videos created by agriculturists) among rural farmers in India.

The databases of these farming videos are created by our internal teams and their management is the most critical part of our work. Currently we use an internally developed technology for video management, that is not very user friendly and intensive on time and effort. We were trying to design an internal survey through which we wanted to know the problems currently faced by our staff in using the current tools.

WHY WE USED THE TOOL:

We used the Question Ladder tool because we wanted to construct some very specific questions as a warm-up and then move to open ended questions that would be complex but more revealing. The responses to this activity would help the software team understand how to make the internal video management activity more effective and efficient.

HOW WE USED THE TOOL:

We used this framework in the worksheet to design questions for an internal survey that we issued to internal programme teams to assess their process of entering data, uploading videos and mapping them. It worked very well because it was straightforward and we were able to design the questionnaire at many different levels of complexity, which we found opened up our line of questioning.

RESULTS OF USING THE TOOL:

We were able to design our survey in a more structured manner. Some example questions that we constructed are:

- Why is it important, or not important, for Digital Green to have a copy of all videos?
- In the future, who might want to create collections on our website?
- Is it likely that someone might forget to link an uploaded video's youtube id in COCO?

Mapping motivations and performance barriers for various stakeholders involved in an employability programme for out-of school youth.

I want to know the people I'm working with by clarifying relationships between stakeholders

▽

PEOPLE & CONNECTIONS MAP

INSPIRED BY
Namahn and Yellow Window Service Design, Design Flanders (2012) Stakeholder Mapping. In: Service design toolkit.

LEVEL OF INVOLVEMENT

MORE COMPLEX TOOL that should ideally be done over a few days. Given the strategic nature of the inputs/outputs, this needs consultations with seniors, peers and ideally needs to be revised after a first pass.

PEOPLE & CONNECTIONS MAP

What is it & why should I do it?

The **People & Connections Map** is a quick and simple way to visualise exactly who you are trying to reach and how. It gives you an overview of all the different individuals and organisations involved in what you do. It allows you to develop a clearer picture of how all the different people and organisations relate both to your work and each other. These might include the people or communities you work directly with; the various bodies from which you receive (or are seeking) funding; or your own peers, local communities and even international support networks.

The People & Connections Map can be a great resource when sharing what you do and how it links together within the community of stakeholders that surround you. This tool is based on the orginal Stakeholder Spidergram developed by the Helsinki Design Lab, and further inspired by the Stakeholder Mapping tool by Namahn and Yellow Window.

HOW TO USE IT

Start by noting down your target audience, including beneficiaries, users or customers who would benefit from your work, in the centre of the worksheet. Then work your way from the centre towards the outer layers, mapping other people and organisations that are related to the work you do. These could be people and organisations that are responsible alongside you for implementing or delivering your work.

By organising the people and organisations that are related to your work across the concentric circles, you can indicate which of them are closer or farther away from the target audience. The closer to the core, the more influential they are. The closer to the outside, the farther away they are.

In addition it helps to further organise the people and organisations on the map by clustering them in sections that express specific networks, sectors or interest areas. For instance a section with all the people and organisations involved with health, safety, environment or education. Choose sections that are relevant to your situation.

Once the worksheet has been filled, go through each person and organisation on the map with your team and, if necessary, reposition them into the circle and section that the team agrees fits most. This review will give you a useful starting point to discuss which relationships or connections are key, and which may need extra attention. By clearly marking out these fields in the map you can highlight and communicate the main focus for your work.

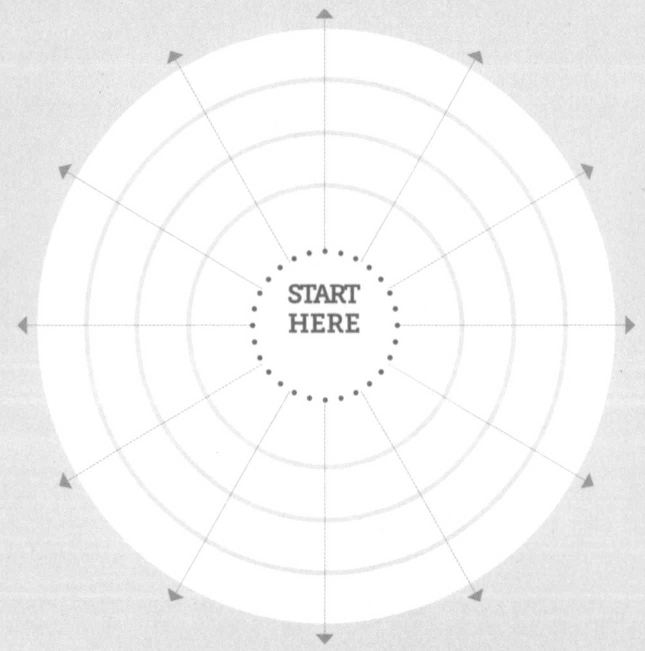

I want to know the people I'm working with
by clarifying relationships between stakeholders

PEOPLE & CONNECTIONS MAP

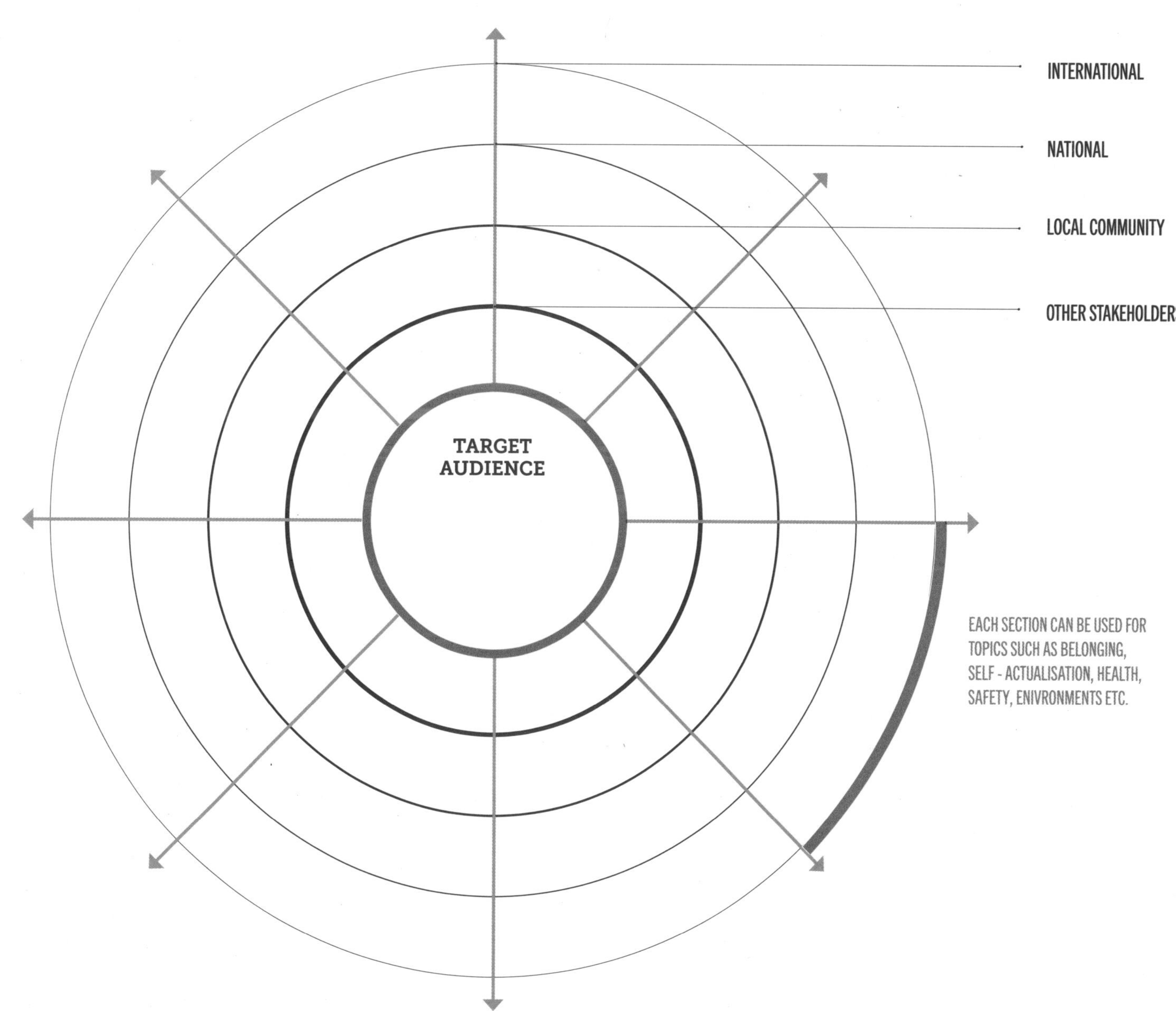

Understanding special hand-washing needs and behaviours for specific user groups living in urban slums.

I want to know the people I'm working with by better defining who I am trying to reach

▽

TARGET GROUP

INSPIRED BY
Nesta (2009) Worksheet 3a: Your Customers. In: Creative Enterprise Toolkit.

LEVEL OF INVOLVEMENT

MORE COMPLEX TOOL that should ideally be done over a few days. Given the strategic nature of the inputs/outputs, this needs consultations with seniors, peers and ideally needs to be revised after a first pass.

What is it & why should I do it?

How to gain better insight into the groups of people you want to cater to, and the kind of needs they have, is a fundamental question for every project or organisation. This tool is a quick and easy way to work out an overview and develop an understanding of the different people your work might reach, and the resources you need to do so.

Target Group is probably best used when you are trying to work out some initial ideas about who you want to cater to, and why. It is also a nice and effective way to share this information with others.

HOW TO USE IT

Fill out the worksheet by considering the needs of the people or organisations you are catering to. Continue with adding notes to describe the potential groups that may be interested in your work, or who may benefit from it. Also try to think about other people or organisations who might also benefit from, or have interests/needs that can be connected to your work. These could be different from your customers.

You can fill out different worksheets for different groups. By using this worksheet you can build a picture of the potential groups of beneficiaries. Do try to also fill out the more exact fields at the bottom. This will help you to get a more concrete sense of the figures involved.

It is useful to add names or brief descriptors for each of the beneficiary groups. If you don't have a name already, think of one that represents the group in a useful way for your organisation. Naming these groups makes it more easy to discuss with your team or other stakeholders. You can do this informally, for instance with friends or colleagues. You can also do it more formally, as part of a meeting with partners or investors. Ideally you could also talk to your customers and other beneficiairies who are in contact with your work, so you can check your assumptions.

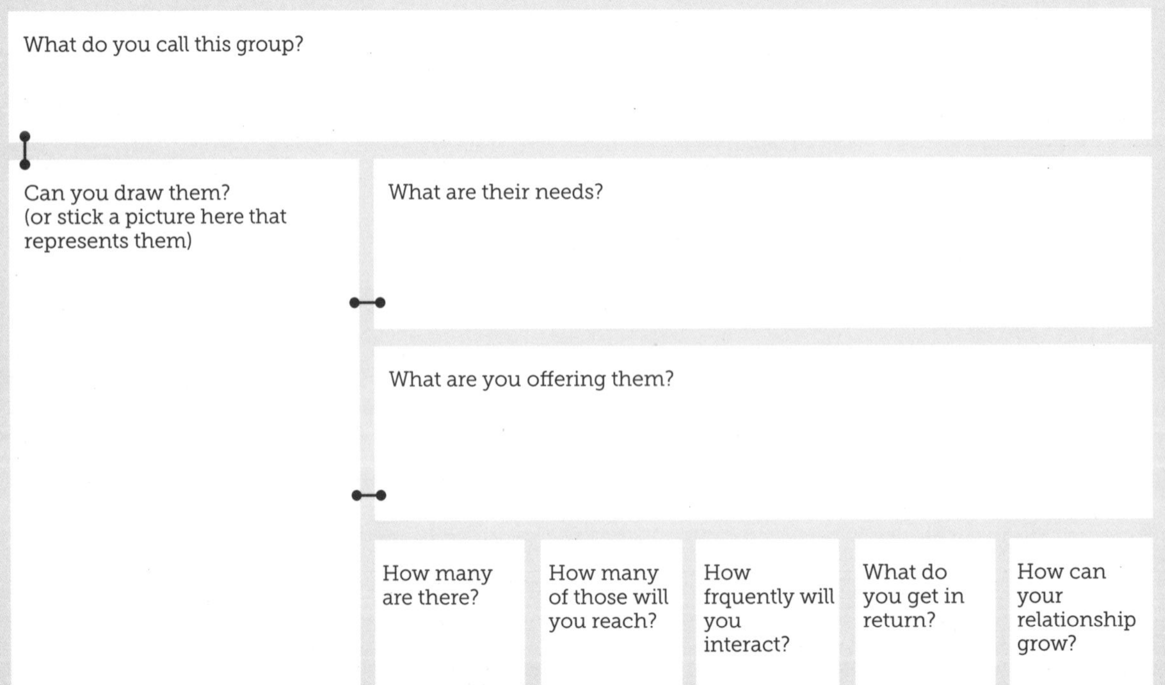

I want to know the people I'm working with
by better defining who I am trying to reach

TARGET GROUP

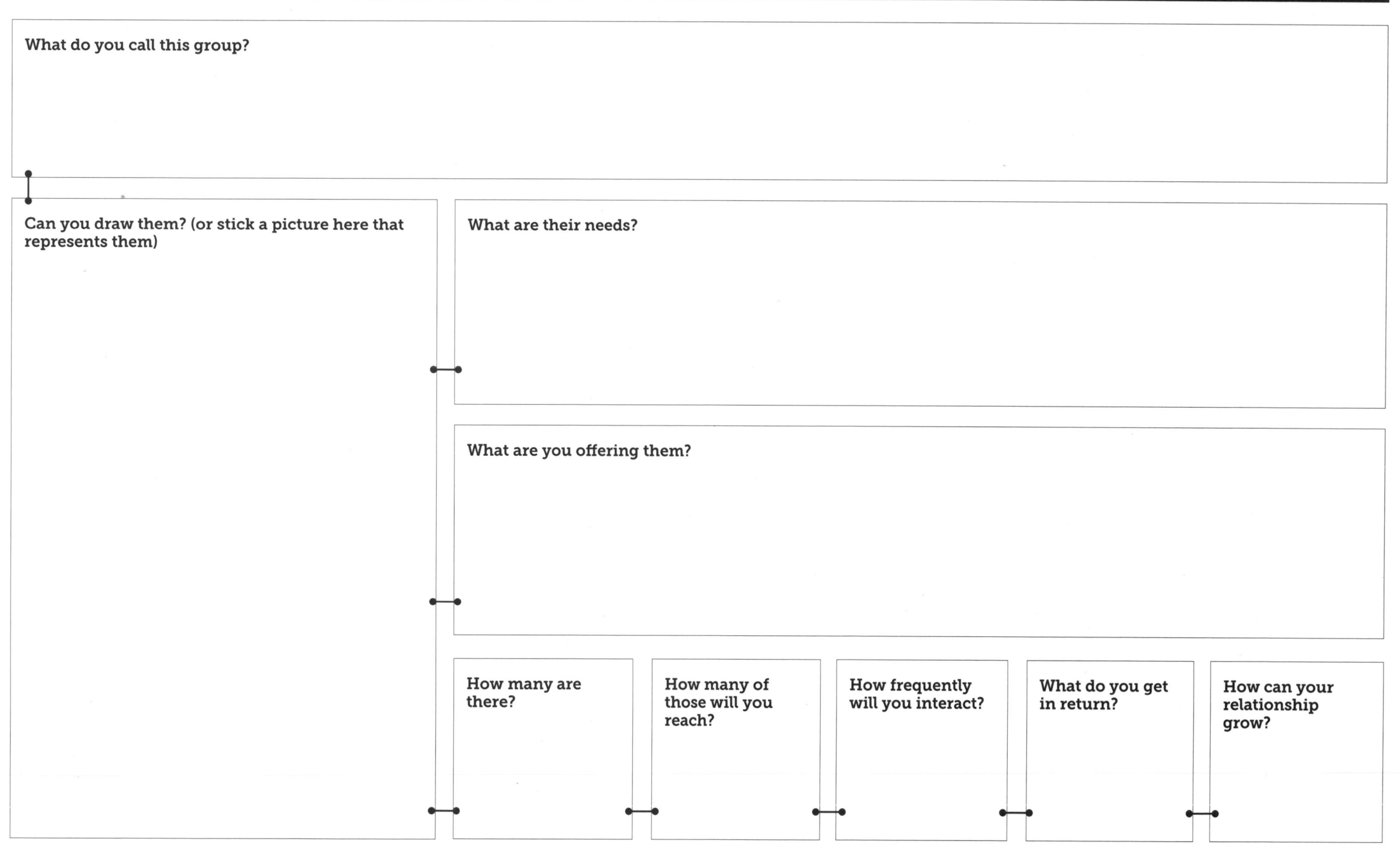

BUSY BEES
Driven by the practicalities of an overloaded everyday life, these are cost-sensitive and eco-aware but neither are crucial factors to them. Focused on their families, jobs and homes, associated practical activities drive their day to day life - water usage is not a priority that defines their lifestyle.
In your daily round, you have plenty of other things to think about apart from water.
If they could show me how much I could have saved over the last five years, then I'd say 'briliant, install the meter tomorrow!'

I want to know the people I'm working with by visualising their key characteristics

▽

PERSONAS

INSPIRED BY
Business Design Toolkit (2010) Personas.

LEVEL OF INVOLVEMENT

REQUIRES SOME DIALOGUE with colleagues/peers. Plan for some time to interact and fill out in collaboration over a day maybe.

PERSONAS

What is it & why should I do it?

Personas are portraits of fictional but realistic individuals that are used as a common reference point to communicate particular groups in your intended audience. Personas are created by drawing together the characteristics of similar people - their behaviours, motivations and the like - into one 'archetype' through which the group can be understood. By creating a fictional character to embody these characteristics, you don't lose the little details that make someone the person they are. In this way, Personas help ensure that your work stays focused on people, rather than an abstract description of the group they are said to represent.

Developing successful Personas is all about knowing what to put in, and what to leave out. They're often developed from a range of different sources, each of which might contain huge amounts of detail. The trick is to recognise the common characteristics that could form the basis of a Persona, and what selection of personal details to include in order to bring this 'to life'. Doing this right can be hugely beneficial as it lets you brainstorm ideas and test potential solutions from their perspective. Often its handy to create a number of Personas so that you can focus on the key characteristics of each subgroup of your intended audience.

? HOW TO USE IT

Personas represent different target subgroups that an organisation wants to reach out to. Being aware of the different preferences, routines and motivations these different Personas have, can help you customise your products and services to these specific subgroups.

Use the worksheet to compile a portrait of a typical person that could represent one of the Personas your organisation is targeting. Try to make the Persona as close to a typical person as possible by adding a name and a picture and descriptions of interests, skills and motivations.

Feel free to add any other details that are relevant to your situation and in relation to this Persona.

ADD PICTURE OR DRAWING Persona name: Audience segment:	Who am I?	3 reasons for me to engage with you 1. 2. 3.	3 reasons for me not to engage with you 1. 2. 3.	
My interests	My personality	My skills	My dreams	My social environment

I want to know the people I'm working with
by visualising their key characteristics

PERSONAS

ADD PICTURE OR DRAWING

Persona name:

Audience segment:

Who am I?

3 reasons for me to engage with you

1.

2.

3.

3 reasons for me not to engage with you

1.

2.

3.

My interests

My personality

My skills

My dreams

My social environment

Envisioning offerings for 'More than a Job', an employability platform for young people.

I want to know the people I'm working with by defining how my offering is new to them

PROMISES & POTENTIAL MAP

INSPIRED BY
IDEO (2011) Deliver: Plan a pipeline of solutions, p135. In: IDEO, Human Centered Design Toolkit. Edition - 2. London: IDEO.

LEVEL OF INVOLVEMENT

REQUIRES SOME DIALOGUE with colleagues/peers. Plan for some time to interact and fill out in collaboration over a day maybe.

PROMISES & POTENTIAL MAP

What is it & why should I do it?

The **Promises & Potential Map** is a simple way to define your added value by mapping the relationship between what you do and who you do it for. The tool provides a diagram on which you can plot each idea or solution you are developing, whether it is targeted at people you work with already, or people you'd like to start reaching out to. Each idea is also classified as being completely new, or something that builds upon what you do already. In this way any potential new solutions you develop are mapped alongside the promises you've already made - and you can see how both relate to the people who might be affected.

Sometimes mapping things out in this way is useful for understanding how much work - and how much benefit - a potential solution might bring. In this worksheet, which has been inspired by Users & Offerings (IDEO 2011), you can map which ideas and offerings are radically new and which are based on existing ones.

HOW TO USE IT

For both axes independently, first decide where a specific offering by you or your organisation is positioned. Is it a new or existing offering? Is it for new or existing users? Then find a spot on the map where these two positions cross - that is where you place the particular idea.

Depending on where your offering ends up, you'll get a sense of whether it is disruptive or building on something existing i.e. incremental. This can help to understand whether you are taking a high risk by doing something radically new, or a low risk by building on what is already there.

Your offering can have several sub-offerings, and each of these can represent a different position on the map. Using the tool gives you a sense of the spread of your portfolio.

This can be potentially used as an interesting way to brainstorm ideas - and help you prioritise them into a product development pipeline for your organisation.

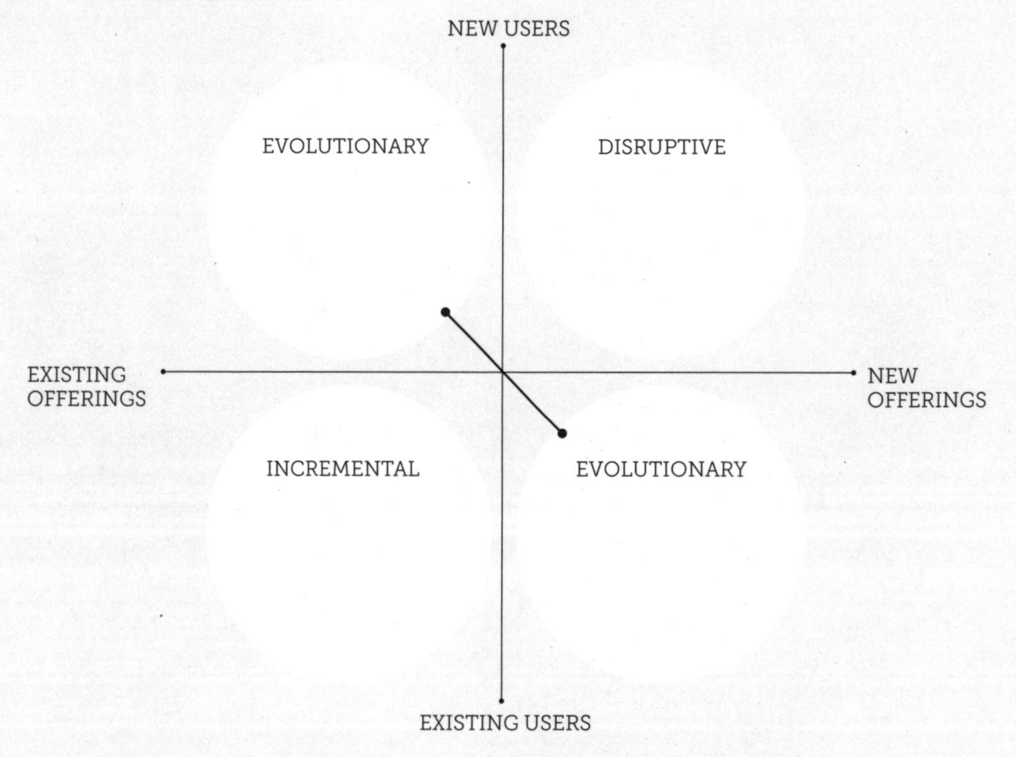

I want to know the people I'm working with
by defining how my offering is new to them

PROMISES & POTENTIAL MAP

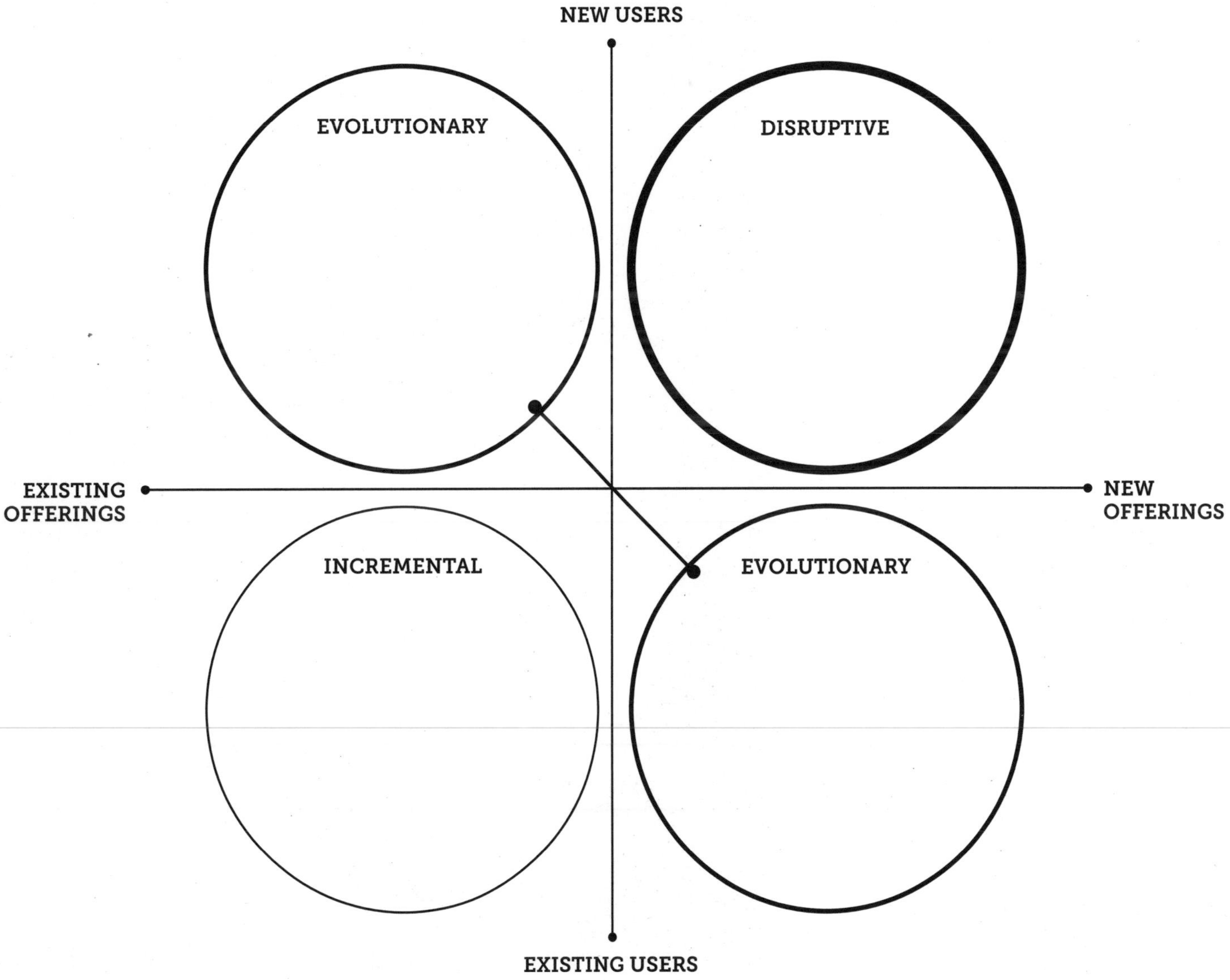

NEW USERS

EVOLUTIONARY

DISRUPTIVE

EXISTING OFFERINGS

NEW OFFERINGS

INCREMENTAL

EVOLUTIONARY

EXISTING USERS

TOOL USED: TARGET GROUP, PERSONAS

ORGANISATION: UNDP UZBEKISTAN

COUNTRY: UZBEKISTAN

SECTOR: COMMUNITY OUTREACH / EDUCATION

ROLE: COMMUNITY OUTREACH SPECIALIST

PROJECT: UNDP/UN VOLUNTEERS JOINT PROJECT 'SOCIAL INNOVATION AND VOLUNTEERISM IN UZBEKISTAN

CONTACT PERSON: ANDREAS KARPATI

EMAIL: ANDREAS.KARPATI@UNDP.ORG

Development Fund of Children's Sport Under the Ministry of Public Education in Uzbekistan was concerned that despite a large-scale investment programme into sports complexes, the use of these facilities has been below expectations, especially outside Tashkent (the capital of Uzbekistan).

The Children's Sports Fund is particularly concerned about the participation of girls from rural areas in sports, who often miss out on the benefits of doing sports due to a lack of parental awareness, encouragement or even permission.

So, despite major investments into infrastructure and programmes guaranteeing free access to sports facilities, how do we get people to use the facilities?

TARGET GROUP AND PERSONAS WORKSHEETS FILLED BY THE WORKSHOP PARTICIPANTS.

WHY WE USED THE TOOL:

We organised a workshop on social innovation with young citizens - students from a local partner university, focused on the 'sport for social inclusion'. Promising project proposals that come out of this, were eligible to be considered for a small grant award of up to $1,500. While making these project proposals, we used a number of tools such as Target Group, Personas to think about the users and Problem Definition, Causes Diagram to think about possible problems and solutions.

The tools were chosen along three main criteria:

1. Suitability for small-scale volunteer projects without commercial elements.
2. Applicable for the early, pre-prototyping stage of social innovation process (emphasis on ideation, problem definition, working out users).
3. Can be carried out in less than an hour in a classroom/workshop setting.

HOW WE USED THE TOOL:

The Target Group and Personas tools were helpful in making the students think about the detailed characteristics of their future users. They often talked about 'heads of traditional families' for example, but the tools helped them to anchor such generalisations in concrete characteristics: where are they to be found, what do they do on an average day, what concrete values do they hold, what media do they consume, what is their relationship with modern technology, etc. We used this tool to highlight the characteristics of our target customers by 'putting ourselves in the other person's shoes.'

We realised that no problem can be solved without taking into consideration the personality of people, their needs and a holistic picture of their lives.

RESULTS OF USING THE TOOL:

We realised that no problem can be solved without taking into consideration the personality of people, their needs and a holistic picture of their lives.

Tips for other people:

- It is better not to concentrate on one type of personality for the Personas tool and instead create multiple Personas, because the problem can cover different social groups.
- Its wise to prepare and collect some data before using the Target your Audience tools in a workshop setting.

 DIY

CASE STUDY

TOOL USED: PERSONAS

ORGANISATION: UNDP KOSOVO

COUNTRY: KOSOVO

SECTOR: LOCAL GOVERNANCE

ROLE: PROJECT MANAGER, SOCIAL MEDIA FOR INNOVATIVE LOCAL EMPOWERMENT

CONTACT PERSON: LEJLA SADIKU

EMAIL: LEJLA.SADIKU@UNDP.ORG

FURTHER INFORMATION: HTTP://WWW.UNDP.ORG/CONTENT/KOSOVO/EN/HOME/OPERATIONS/PROJECTS/DEMOCRATIC_GOVERNANCE/SMILE.HTML

My team and I are working on a project seeking to build bridges between decision makers and young people.

One such project with UNWomen, involves a series of discussions on Twitter with female role models in politics. One predicament for us is that of understanding our audience better and being specific about who we are trying to reach through these interventions. And hence we used the Personas tool.

HOW WE USED THE TOOL:

We workshopped the tool with 6 people for 2.5 hours. Everyone worked individually in constructing a persona with very little moderation. Through the exercise we quickly established that we needed to engage with people outside of our digital audience; a wider group of activists and students working on gender issues that we don't normally interact with. In smaller municipalities people are far less conversant with Twitter and so we identified a real need to engage users through other methods, Facebook for instance, or even Twitter Lunch Cafes - where people people can come together in an offline space and be assisted in bringing their issues to a virtual discussion.

RESULTS OF USING THE TOOL:

The tool was extremely useful in helping us narrow down our core audiences for this initiative and to understand some of the obstacles that they might face in joining an online discussion.

We gained more clarity about our outreach activities needing to blend offline and online events, and how a part of it should start with universities and spread through student governments.

I want to generate new ideas by working together with people who experience and solve problems

▽

CREATIVE WORKSHOP

INSPIRED BY
Lovlie L.,Reason B.,Polaine A. (2013) Service Design: From Insight to Implementation. p60. Rosenfeld Media.

LEVEL OF INVOLVEMENT

REQUIRES SOME DIALOGUE with colleagues/peers. Plan for some time to interact and fill out in collaboration over a day maybe.

CREATIVE WORKSHOP

What is it & why should I do it?

A **Creative Workshop** is an opportunity to bring together and collaborate with a number of different people involved with or affected by your work. They might include the people you're trying to reach, the partners you're working with, experts brought in from similar fields, or any combination of these (and other) groups who would benefit from talking to each other. It is a good way to both collect and share different experiences, as well as co-create potential solutions.

Creative Workshops can provide invaluable insights into people's perspectives on particular issues. And they offer a setting where this knowledge is shared as soon as it's gathered. Structuring sessions that involve different people from several different backgrounds however is something that needs careful planning. This tool provides a checklist for planning your session effectively, helping you make the most of the group dynamics.

HOW TO USE IT

Creative workshops can have different purposes:

- Generating and exploring a range of ideas
- Selecting and building upon the best ideas
- Creating a clear vision for how the ideas can be made real at a later stage

A clear step-by-step schedule of activities, and timings for each activity will help make the workshop a success. It is important to plan your workshop well.

Here are some points to consider while planning one:

- How long will the workshop be, and where will it take place?
- Who will attend the workshop, and what is the mix of knowledge and skills?
- What will be the schedule for the day?
- Will you be working in small groups? How will they share their ideas?
- What materials and tools are you intending to use?
- How will you document the results?

The following worksheet is only one example of how a Creative Workshop can be conducted. Depending on your needs/constraints, feel free to modify (add/subtract/reorder) each time you plan a workshop.

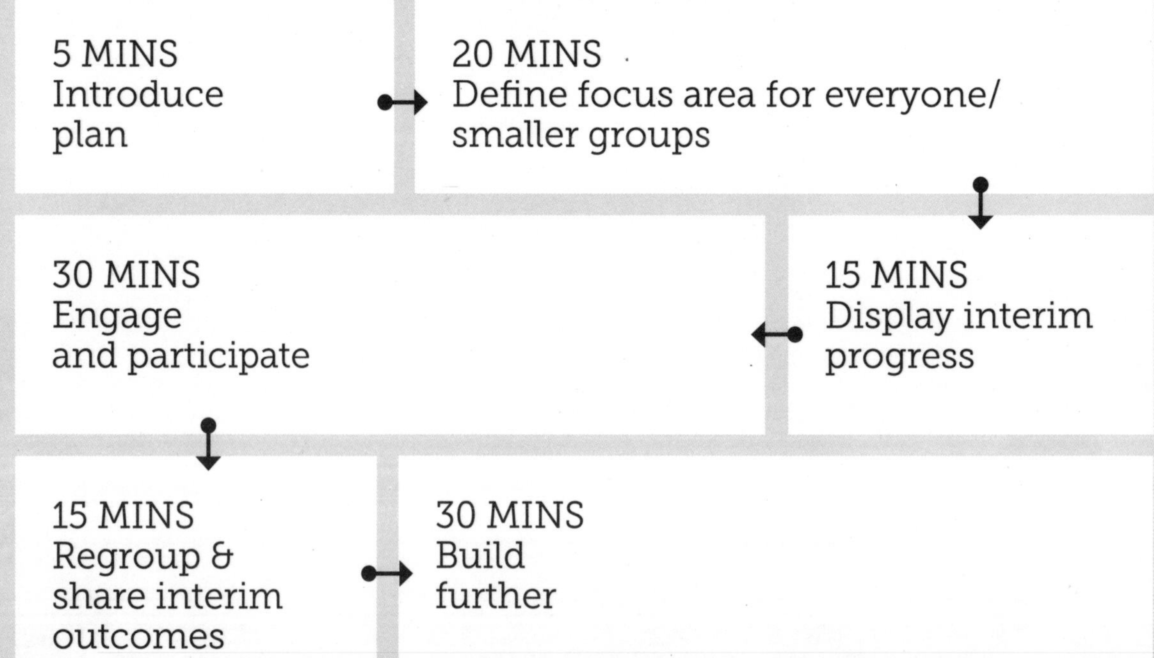

I want to generate new ideas
by working together with people who experience and solve problems

CREATIVE WORKSHOP

5 MINS
Introduce the workshop plan

20 MINS
Define who the session is focused on
(eg. Work in small groups on creating personas)

15 MINS
Put these up on a wall where everyone can see them.

30 MINS
Define how the target user will make use of your offering
(eg. Create a journey map for each persona)

15 MINS
Share the outcomes of the journey map with the rest of the teams.
Share opportunities where the group thinks it can create or add value.

30 MINS
Further build on the opportunities identified by tools you used
(eg. Promises & Potential Map, Business Model Canvas, Theory Of Change)

Working together to generate possible solutions at a workshop.

I want to generate new ideas by thinking differently

FAST IDEA GENERATOR

INSPIRED BY
Nesta (2013) Fast Idea Generator

LEVEL OF INVOLVEMENT

FAIRLY SIMPLE, SELF ADMINISTERED TOOL
needs relatively less time.

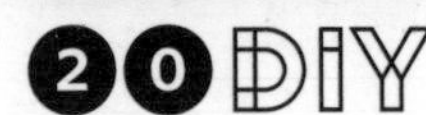

FAST IDEA GENERATOR

What is it & why should I do it?

This tool allows a team to generate ideas by looking at a problem or opportunity from a range of perspectives. This helps come up with new ideas for potential solutions, and also strengthens current offerings, as it challenges it from different approaches. Comprised of seven approaches, or challenges, you can choose the ones that seem most applicable to take the topic at hand further, thus using the tool to inspire further discussions.

The **Fast Idea Generator** helps frame ideas, problems or opportunities in relation to different scenarios. It stretches the thinking around a concept in different directions, providing a stimulating discussion that will further strengthen the concept. To use the tool effectively, the starting point (problem, opportunity, concept idea or existing proposition) should be clearly laid out.

HOW TO USE IT

Step 1 is to start from an existing concept, problem or opportunity and then apply the seven challenges suggested in the worksheet. These are simple steps to help come up with alternatives that bend, break and stretch the 'normal rules' in such a way that you can generate many surprising ideas in a short period of time.

Step 2 is then to review the ideas and select the best ones to further flesh them out into workable innovations.

THE APPROACH		THE NORMAL RULE	BENDING, BREAKING & STRETCHING THE RULE
Inversion	Turn common practice upside down		
Integration	Integrate the offer with other offers		
Extension	Extend the offer		
Differentiation	Segment the offer		
Addition	Add a new element		
Subtraction	Take something away		
Translation	Translate a practice associated with another field		
Grafting	Graft on an element of practice from another field		
Exaggeration	Push something to its most extreme expression		

I want to generate new ideas
by thinking differently

FAST IDEA GENERATOR

THE APPROACH		THE NORMAL RULE	BENDING, BREAKING & STRETCHING THE RULE
Inversion	Turn common practice upside down	Doctors treat patients	What if patients became doctors?
Integration	Integrate the offer with other offers	People access a range of services in different locations	What if different local services had one point of access?
Extension	Extend the offer	Schools provide learning opportunities to children and young people during the day	What if schools also offered sport and recreation; and community learning after hours?
Differentiation	Segment the offer	There is a 'one size fits all' approach	What if a service was personalised and differently segmented?
Addition	Add a new element	Supermarkets deliver groceries	What if supermarkets delivered groceries and also provided hot meals to older people in their homes?
Subtraction	Take something away	Prisons are critical to an effective criminal justice system	What if you had to close three prisons?
Translation	Translate a practice associated with another field	Hospitals and airports are different kinds of operations	What if airport management practices were applied to hospitals?
Grafting	Graft on an element of practice from another field	Teaching and coaching are separate practices	What if coaching was introduced as part of secondary school education?
Exaggeration	Push something to its most extreme expression	Schools support children and young people to learn, but only within designated times and in a designated space	What if students could access learning, anytime and anywhere they chose?

Discussing ideas and their wider impact for an 'earn and learn' programme for underprivileged youth

I want to generate new ideas by framing a constructive discussion with my team

THINKING HATS

INSPIRED BY
de Bono, E. (1985) Six Thinking Hats. USA: Little, Brown and Company.

LEVEL OF INVOLVEMENT

REQUIRES SOME DIALOGUE with colleagues/peers. Plan for some time to interact and fill out in collaboration over a day maybe.

THINKING HATS

What is it & why should I do it?

Thinking Hats allow a range of different viewpoints and perspectives to be brought into a discussion, whilst keeping the focus on the issue at hand. It's a technique which can be used to encourage people to look at a topic from a number of different perspectives, making what might be a very complex issue, a stimulating focus point for conversation. The team learns how to separate thinking into six clear functions and roles, getting them to look at all sides of an issue. Structuring the conversation around these different viewpoints helps avoid endless, free flowing debates around topics, and instead helps create a meaningful, focused discussion. This technique was popularised in the book Six Thinking Hats (De Bono E. 1985).

Each hat is a different theme, which indicates a particular viewpoint. In a group setting all team members think about a topic using the range of hats, helping them focus on the topic one viewpoint at a time. This also helps getting contributions from all team members. The range of viewpoints can uncover new ways to address a particularly difficult problem, for instance by making an overly familiar issue feel 'strange' again, and it helps teams develop a shared understanding.

HOW TO USE IT

There are two ways of using the Thinking Hats:

1. Everyone 'wears' the same hat at the same time. Choose one of the hats and ask everyone to contribute to the discussion from that hat's point of view. Each of the six hats is used to discuss an issue.

2. Everyone 'wears' a different hat and the topic is discussed from multiple points of view. All hats need to contribute sufficiently to the discussion. Hats can be switched around during the discussion, forcing people to look at the issue differently.

Both approaches help teams engage in critical discussions. The hats break-up the conversation into focused parts that can be conducted one after the other, instead of simultaneously. There is no correct order for which hat comes first or last, but for the first few times, it may be easiest to use the sequence as indicated on the worksheet (from factual to management).

The use of these hats may seem artificial at first, but once you go through the exercise a few times, the advantage becomes evident.

If 'hats' are not appropriate for the situation just use T-shirts, badges, or cards with the themes of the hats on them.

Factual

Emotional

Logical

Cautious

Out of the box

Management

I want to generate new ideas
by framing a constructive discussion with my team

THINKING HATS

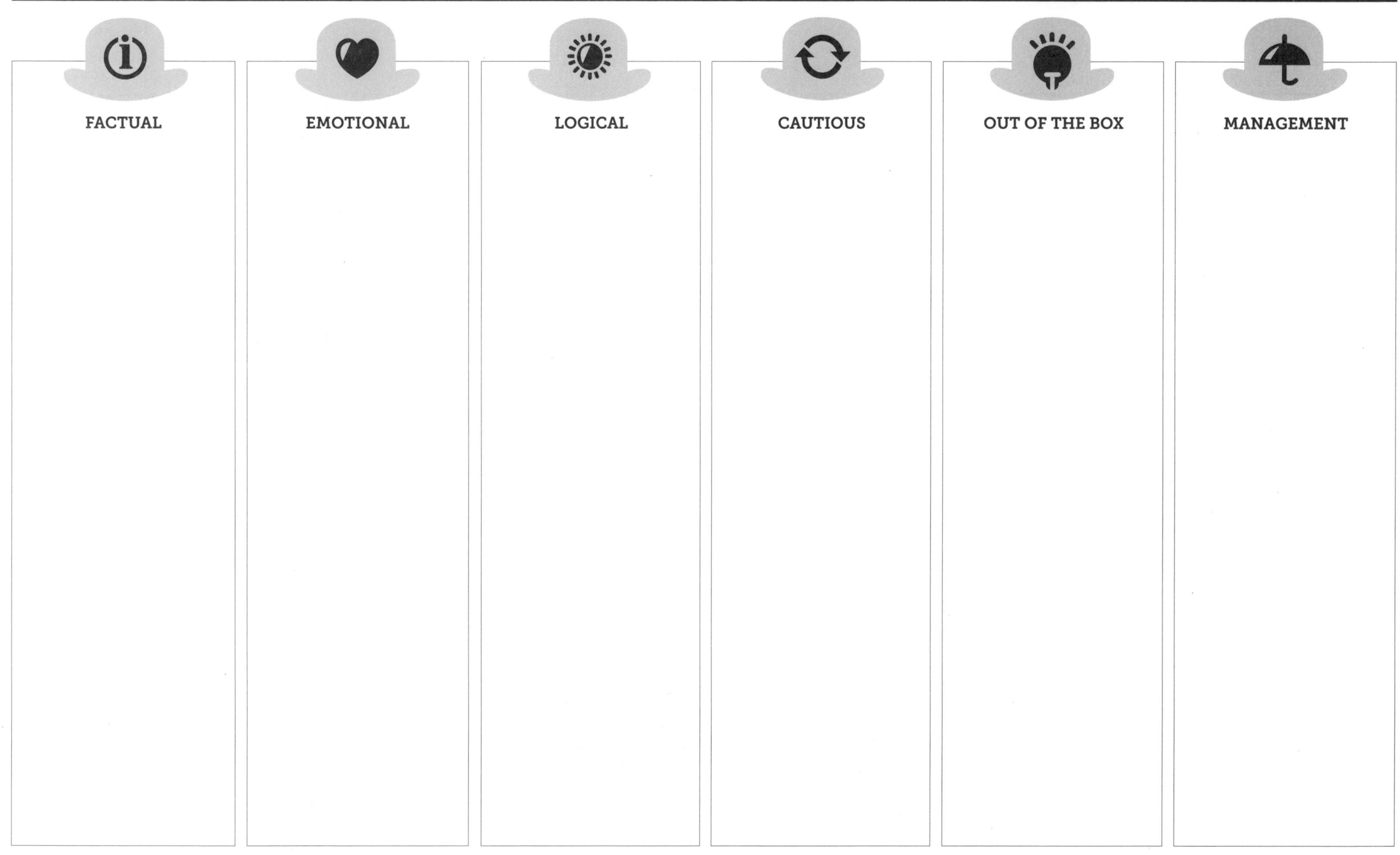

Understanding and prioritising the values embodied by a social business around sanitation services.

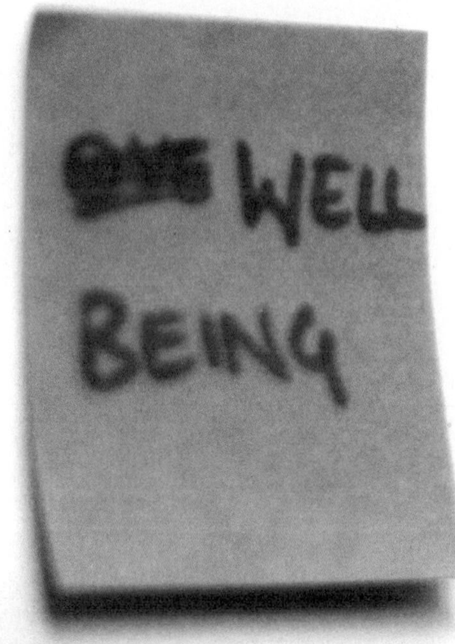

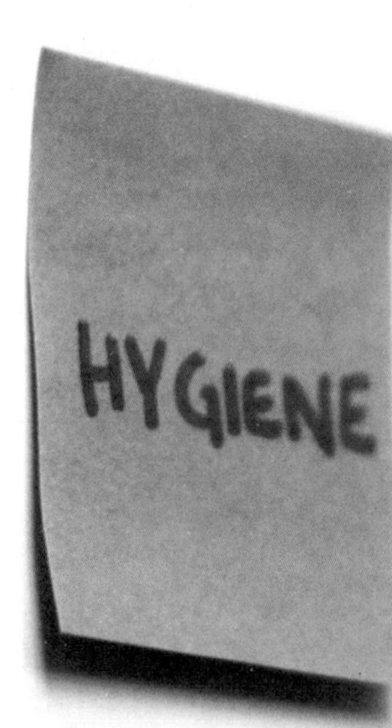

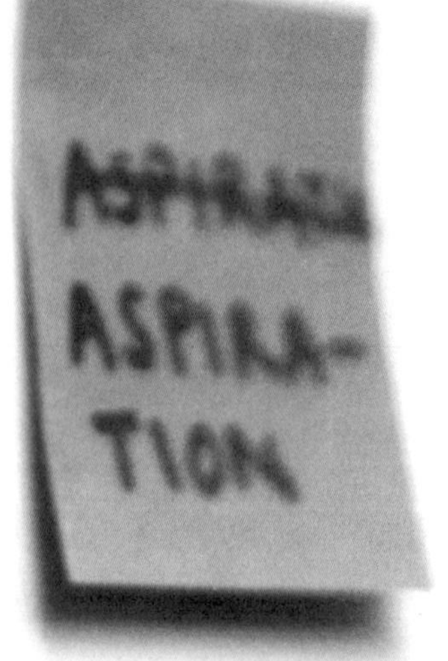

I want to generate new ideas by aligning our work based on shared values

▽

VALUE MAPPING

INSPIRED BY
Nesta (2009) Worksheet 2a: Your Values. In: Creative Enterprise Toolkit.

LEVEL OF INVOLVEMENT

FAIRLY SIMPLE, SELF ADMINISTERED TOOL
needs relatively less time.

What is it & why should I do it?

What makes you do what you do? **Value Mapping** helps you answer this by enabling you to describe the values which are embodied in your personal work and in the wider organisation. These values are probably more influential than anything else in shaping what you do. They might be something that you take for granted, that you think is obvious, or that you've never actually articulated or written down. Defining these values however can be very useful when trying to explain your work to other colleagues and partners.

Once the values are defined, they can be shared and act as a common reference point that simplifies and speeds up decisions, whilst also ensuring consistency in the work that you do. This is a seemingly simple task, but one which can be hugely valuable when done properly - something this worksheet helps you do. It can be especially useful to bring all team members on the same page during projects by having the team first make their personal value maps and then match these with each other.

? HOW TO USE IT

Start by individually writing down on a piece of paper or a series of cards, what you feel is most valuable for yourself as well as for the organisation. Think of these personal values as the things that make you feel truly alive and passionately committed to what you are doing in your organisation. For one person it might be things like helping others, for another it might be creativity or innovation, for someone else it might be honesty, ecological awareness or leadership. Write down a lot of them – even the ones that you are aware of but are less important to you.

When you have noted down a wide range of values (ten or more), place them in the relevant fields on the worksheet. Don't worry about getting it right first time – swap them around until you have them in the right place. To focus your activities, have a maximum of five in the 'Always important' column.

Ask your other team members to do the same. Once all their worksheets have been defined, these can be shared and agreed upon. Showing your completed worksheet to someone who knows you well and asking for their feedback helps clarify what is important to you. Together you can establish what values are important to the organisation as a whole.

Always important	Sometimes important	Rarely important	Never important
INDIVIDUAL VALUES			

Always important	Sometimes important	Rarely important	Never important
ORGANISATION VALUES			

I want to generate new ideas
by aligning our work based on shared values

VALUE MAPPING

INDIVIDUAL VALUES

Always important	Sometimes important	Rarely important	Never important

ORGANISATION VALUES

Always important	Sometimes important	Rarely important	Never important

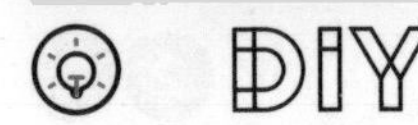

CASE STUDY

TOOL USED: SWOT ANALYSIS, PERSONAS, THINKING HATS

ORGANISATION: HUMANITARIAN STREETMAP

COUNTRY: INDONESIA

SECTOR: OPEN DATA

CONTACT PERSON: KATE CHAPMAN

EMAIL: KATE.CHAPMAN@HOTOSM.ORG

FURTHER INFORMATION: HTTP://EN.OPENSTREETMAP.OR.ID/

We were writing a grant proposal for the Australia-Indonesia Facility for Disaster Reduction (AIFDR) to secure new funding for our 2014 activities. For this, we held an internal strategy meeting that inputs into a larger workshop with partners and stakeholders to solicit feedback on our 2014 plan.

WHY WE USED THE TOOLS:

Our intent was to brainstorm both how we can better service people and groups we currently work with and if there are new ones we have not thought about. Often in such situations, it is easy to get caught in the same line of thinking and not imagine new methods of outreach to different groups. I thought that the Personas and the Thinking Hats would be good ways to do that.

I used the SWOT Analysis also because I felt that I knew my views on our strengths and weaknesses, but not necessarily my team's views. Having a firm understanding of how things stand from someone executing our programme tasks directly is vital.

HOW WE USED THE TOOLS:

In a 5 hour long workshop, we broke into small groups to work through each of the tools and then re-convened to amalgamate our thoughts and sprinkle the new perspectives into elements of the grant proposal. Generally the group work was very positive and hugely beneficial to bring the team together in this manner – more fun than the typical brainstorming we do.

The SWOT Analysis worked really well with the team. After this we used the Personas worksheet - which was especially helpful. We are trying to figure out what changes need to be made to our programme to reach a wider audience, so we tried a couple of personas that weren't our current "customers" and got some great ideas.

With the Thinking Hats though, we hit a bit of trouble. Some of it might have been my explanation. I think if I do it again I would translate the names of the different hats into Indonesian first. Everybody in the team speaks English, but the concept was a bit abstract for them.

RESULTS OF USING THE TOOL:

The activity resulted in clear inputs that were assimilated into a co-written grant proposal. Looking deeper, we have a better sense of some internal processes that we can use to advance our planning documents with our staff and board – so that we can be more intentional about our innovation practice.

Tips for other people:
Culturally adapt the tools to accommodate for varying degrees of English proficiency.

CASE STUDY

TOOL USED: VALUE MAPPING

ORGANISATION: FHI 360

COUNTRY: INDIA

SECTOR: PUBLIC HEALTH, NUTRITION AND WASH

ROLE: TEAM LEADER

CONTACT PERSON: SUBBANAICKER KRISHNASWAMY

EMAIL: SKRISHNASWAMY@MPTAST.ORG

I lead a team of professionals providing Technical Assistance and Support to the Govt of Madhya Pradesh covering the thematic areas of health, nutrition and WASH (Water, sanitation and hygiene). I feel that there are several critical issues that come in the way of effective and efficient management of service delivery, often pushing the actual goal of social development to the background. Broadly classified into two categories - individual and organisational, these issues can be notions of governance, human resource and organisational development.

WHY/HOW WE USED THE TOOL:

I used the Value Mapping tool for identifying core values at the individual and organisational level that can bring a much wanted change in the way the whole system operates. The idea was to try out 'change management' in the system so that the resources are used productively to deliver services like basic health, nutrition and sanitation to the people we cater to.

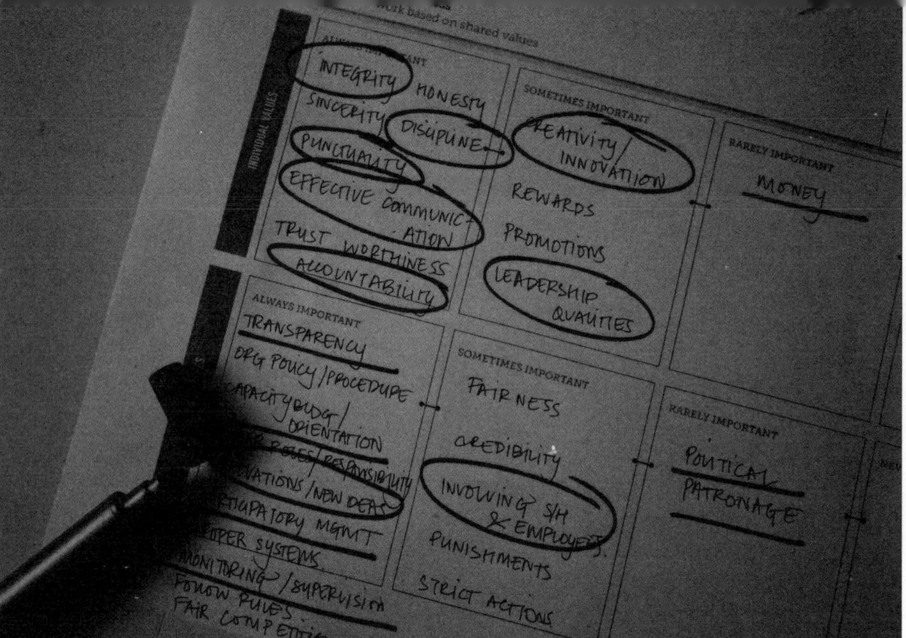

A SNAPSHOT OF THE VALUE MAPPING TOOL FILLED OUT WITH THE TEAM.

> One of the problems we face is the resistance to change, and how the organisation is used to the 'status quo'.

My team drew up an annual work plan covering human resource and organisational development dimensions. Compartmentalising these values into four neat boxes is easier said than done, but in reality they all overlap both at the individual and organisational level. These values change with the personalities occupying the positions at the policy making level and the professionalism of the individual players who are responsible for driving the change.

RESULTS OF USING THE TOOL:

After the exercise, the outputs were shared with the government (who we work very closely with) and we are initiating a buy in from their side.

I want to test & improve by understanding what is most effective in my work

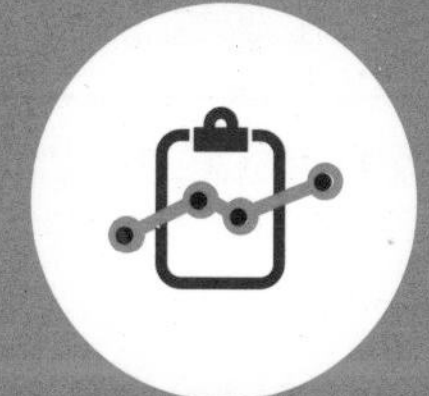

IMPROVEMENT TRIGGERS

INSPIRED BY
Eberle, B (1997) Scamper Worksheet. USA: Prufrock Press.

LEVEL OF INVOLVEMENT

FAIRLY SIMPLE, SELF ADMINISTERED TOOL
needs relatively less time.

IMPROVEMENT TRIGGERS

What is it & why should I do it?

Improvement Triggers provides a collection of questions which can be used to help you look at your work a bit differently. Inspired by the tool 'SCAMPER' (Eberle B. 1997), these questions are designed to provoke you into new ways of thinking, and are structured in a way that lets you approach either your existing offering or a potential new solution from a number of directions. This is a great way to make your work stronger, especially in areas where lots of competing solutions are already available.

The questions in this tool assume that anything new is a modification of something that already exists. This might not always be strictly true, but approaching your work from this perspective can very be useful when you're trying to articulate how what you're doing is different from anyone else (or how it builds on what's gone before).

? HOW TO USE IT

Each of the questions on the worksheet should give a slightly different perspective on your work. Note your answers in the space provided, but try to keep it brief - the idea is to end up with something that will give you a concise overview of how your work is different, and how you could potentially improve it.

The questions on this worksheet are examples to trigger your thinking. Many other questions may be relevant as well. The key is to use the seven categories of questions to provoke thoughts on potential improvements.

Substitute	Combine	Adapt	Modify	Put to another use	Eliminate	Reverse

I want to test and improve
by understanding what is most effective in my work

IMPROVEMENT TRIGGERS

Substitute	Combine	Adapt	Modify	Put to another use	Eliminate	Reverse
What materials or resources can you substitute or swap to improve your work? What other process materials could you use? What rules could you substitute?	What would happen if you combined different aspects of your work, to create something new? What if you combined purposes or objectives? What could you combine to maximise the uptake of your work? How could you combine talent and resources to create a new approach?	How could you adapt or readjust your work to serve another purpose or use? Who or what could you emulate to adapt your work? What other context could you put your work into? What other products or ideas could you use for inspiration?	What could you add to modify your work? What could you emphasise or highlight to create more value? What element of your work could you strengthen to create something new?	Can you use your work somewhere else? Who else could benefit from your work? How else could you do your work - perhaps in another setting? Could you reuse some ideas/things from a previous project?	How could you streamline or simplify your work? What elements of your work could you make more fun? What elements of your work or even rules could you eliminate? What could you have in its place?	What would happen if you reversed your process or sequenced them differently? What if you did the exact opposite of what you're trying to do now? How can you re-organise your work?

Testing architectural layouts with potential users of a new public sanitation facility.

I want to test & improve by collecting useful feedback on my work at different phases

PROTOTYPE TESTING PLAN

INSPIRED BY
Nesta (2011) Prototyping in Public Spaces.

LEVEL OF INVOLVEMENT

REQUIRES SOME DIALOGUE with colleagues/peers. Plan for some time to interact and fill out in collaboration over a day maybe.

What is it & why should I do it?

Prototyping is something we all do in our daily lives when we try out new things - from trying out new recipes while cooking to trying out different routes while going somewhere - it simply involves trying out an idea to see how it can be improved. At work however, prototyping is more than just 'trying out'; it is a structured way to check that you have an efficient and fitting solution or approach before rolling it out or making a big investment in it.

The **Prototype Testing Plan** gives a basic, but useful overview of the different ways in which you can test your work, as well as when to test it. You can build a prototype using various materials, or simply draw or act out your idea. The Prototype Testing Plan also helps structure the testing process. It is most efficient if you go through a structured series of steps. This way you can continually improve your work, while avoiding getting lost once feedback collected starts piling up. The worksheet indicates two periods when it is usually beneficial to test your idea: in the early stage of development, and in the later stages just before full implementation.

? HOW TO USE IT

Prototyping is often carried out in various stages of a process with the aim of either searching for new ideas or testing an existing idea to see whether it works and how to make it better. Prototypes can be made as often as possible. The key is to keep it easy and cheap to build, focusing more on the core offering rather than smooth finishing. Feel free to use what is easily available around you as long as it helps you try out your idea rather than just talking or thinking about it.

Use the worksheet as a basic guide to help plan your prototype tests. Always clearly specify the main idea you want to test out through your prototype. Make sure to note down any learnings on how to improve your work by reallocating activities, resources, people or materials.

Idea → Try → Test → Specify

I want to test and improve
by collecting useful feedback on my work at different phases

PROTOTYPE TESTING PLAN

Hypothesis

Specify the main idea/ hypothesis that you want to test.

Quickly try out your idea to judge whether it can work in real life.

Build a small model of your idea using cardboard/ paper, children's blocks, toys or any material you see lying around. This is so you can see your idea in three dimensions and check whether it would work smoothly or has gaps.

Act out parts of your idea when you meet with your target audience. Pretend that your idea is launched. How will they know of it and use it? You can use the Experience Map as a guide. Try acting out different possibilities to learn about alternative ways of doing things.

Draw the experience of finding out and using your work in the form of a story to see if you've not missed any step.

Test your idea again after having developed it further, to examine details before launching it.

Build a new model of your idea. Since you have developed your idea further, you should now have more details and elements in it to test and check whether they all work in synchronisation.

Act out your idea again. You can use the Blueprint as a guide to check whether the different elements are matching up properly?

Again draw the experience of using your work in more detail than before. Test out if all the steps in your story are working well together.

Make a list of all the things that you need to make your idea real.

List things like activities, resources, people and materials that you need to make your idea realistic enough to implement.

Working out and sharing a new service idea with the rest of the team.

Global Service Jam London 2013

I want to test & improve by creating an overview of how I engage with my stakeholders

▽

EXPERIENCE MAP

INSPIRED BY
Schneider J., Stickdorn M., (2010)The Customer Journey Canvas. In: This is Service Design Thinking. Amsterdam: BIS Publishers.

LEVEL OF INVOLVEMENT

REQUIRES SOME DIALOGUE with colleagues/peers. Plan for some time to interact and fill out in collaboration over a day maybe.

EXPERIENCE MAP

What is it & why should I do it?

The **Experience Map** allows you to see your work through the eyes of the people receiving, benefitting or even funding it. It lays out the different routes and points at which these people become aware of, connect with, and feel about what you do - especially at the points they come directly in contact with your work. Identifying these junctures, and highlighting the interactions, helps you reflect on how you engage with these people and take your work further.

The worksheet provided here shows how you can quickly define the points which determine different people's perception of what you do - as well as the problems and opportunities each of these moments represent. A completed Experience Map is a way to condense complex information into a format more easily understood, through highlighting key points of your offering.

HOW TO USE IT

Use the worksheet to document experiences from people who have been in contact with your work. Fill out one worksheet per person you have spoken with - the most rich information on this tends to come from interviews.

Capture their activities as well as their motivations and satisfaction. Be sensitive to 'why' as much as to 'what' and 'how'.

Once you have collected a series of Experience Maps based on accounts from various people, you can make comparisons across this set to conclude what recurrent issues people have in the expectations and experiences with your service. Using this tool makes the process of testing more efficient, and improves the quality of how people experience your work.

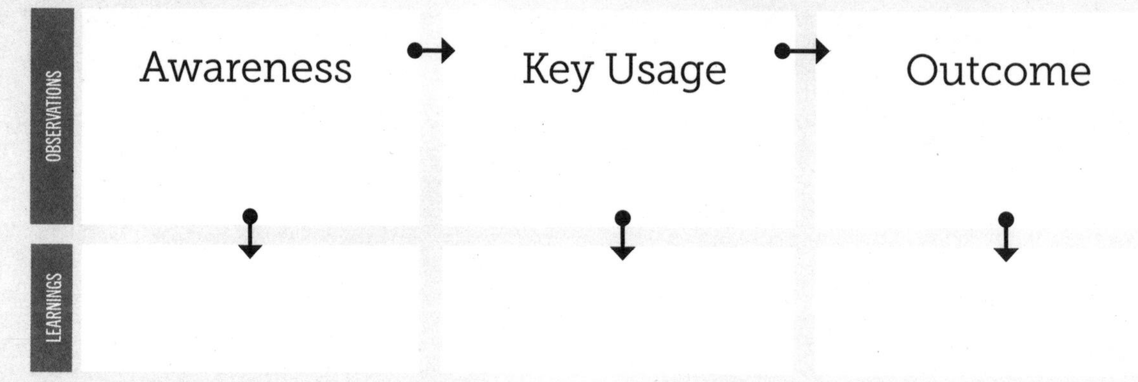

I want to test and improve
by creating an overview of how I engage with my stakeholders

EXPERIENCE MAP

OBSERVATIONS

Awareness

How did this person hear about you? (E.G. PR, social media, word of mouth)
What relevant previous experience did he or she have?

Key usage

What points of contact happened between you and this person?
What were the critical moments, such as especially good or bad experiences?

Outcome

What was the feedback from this person? (eg. via social media or word of mouth)
Was there any follow up from your side?

LEARNINGS

Planning internal and external activities for a conference on art, design and culture.

I want to test & improve by crafting a detailed overview of our operations and resources

BLUEPRINT

INSPIRED BY
The Social Design Methods Menu: Julier J., Kimbell L. (2012) Blueprint. p44.

LEVEL OF INVOLVEMENT

REQUIRES SOME DIALOGUE with colleagues/peers. Plan for some time to interact and fill out in collaboration over a day maybe.

What is it & why should I do it?

A **Blueprint** gives an overview of an organisation's operations, such as key activities, products, services, and points of interaction with the intended audience, stakeholders and beneficiaries. Blueprints help make explicit how existing resources can be repurposed or recycled, and what new resources will be needed. They also give a sense of the overall impact your activities might have. This is highly useful when trying to plan or improve your work.

Filling in the worksheet helps break down your work into smaller details. It provides structure to this analysis by showing a 'line of interaction'. This line represents the distinction between the activities of the intended audience, beneficiaries and other stakeholders, and the activities that take place within your organisation.

? HOW TO USE IT

You can start creating a Blueprint at any point on the worksheet, by filling out key aspects of the interactions between your organisation and its audience or other beneficiaries. The stages at the top of the page represent the stages the interaction with your audience may go through over time (engagement, hand over, use period, follow up). The blocks at the left represent both the external activities by the people you interact with and the internal activities of your team. The 'line of interaction' marks the distinction between external and internal activities.

At the bottom of the page, note down which activities are done internally by your team while they are interacting with your audience. Briefly describe who does what and why, and also what instruments or systems they use for this. At the top of the page,note down which activities are done externally by the people your organisation interacts with, and describe in a similar way who does what and why, and what instruments they may be using for that. From le to right consider which of these activities, actors and instrumen are typical for the various stages. By mapping this out you ca generate an overview of your key activities, the resources neede and how these are related.

Completing the worksheet forces you to think through the differer ingredients involved in creating, communicating and providing you service or product. You can use the worksheet to analyse a curren or future situation. In either case, the worksheet helps you highligh key resources and processes that are required, and to link these wit the people or organisations involved. Try to produce a blueprint fror the perspective of different stakeholders you are working with an anticipate what their activities and responses to your work might b

TIME →

		ENGAGEMENT	→ HANDOVER	→ USE PERIOD	→ SIGN OFF
EXTERNAL ACTIVITIES	Things,media and devices being used				
	What people do, feel, know and think				
↔					
INTERNAL ACTIVITIES	What people in the team do, feel, know and think				
	Supporting instruments and systems used				

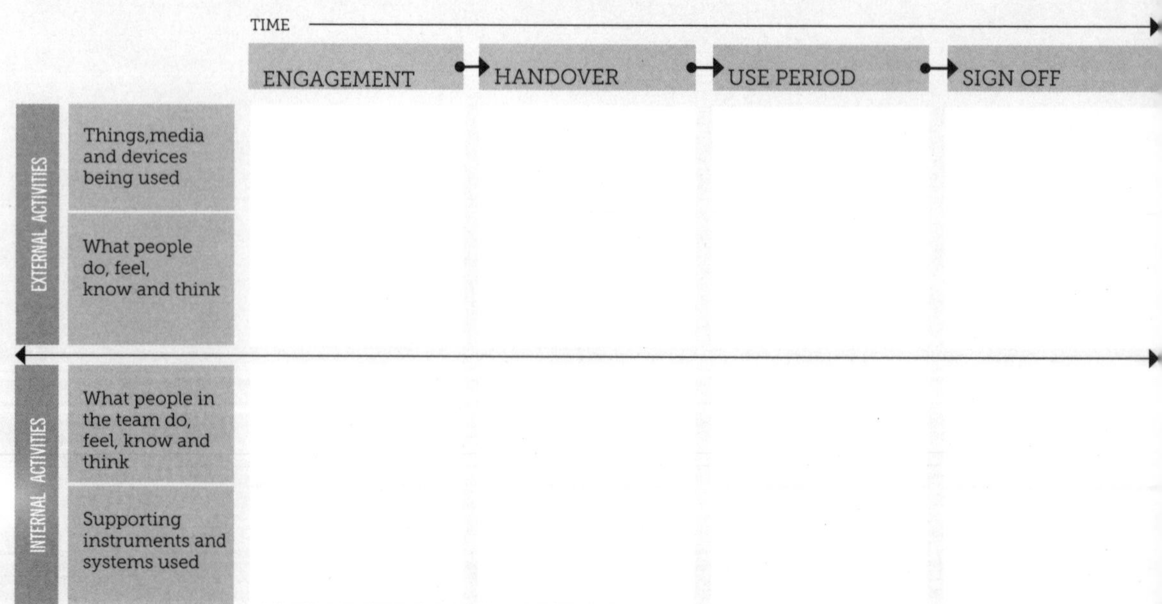

I want to test and improve
by crafting a detailed overview of our operations and resources

BLUEPRINT

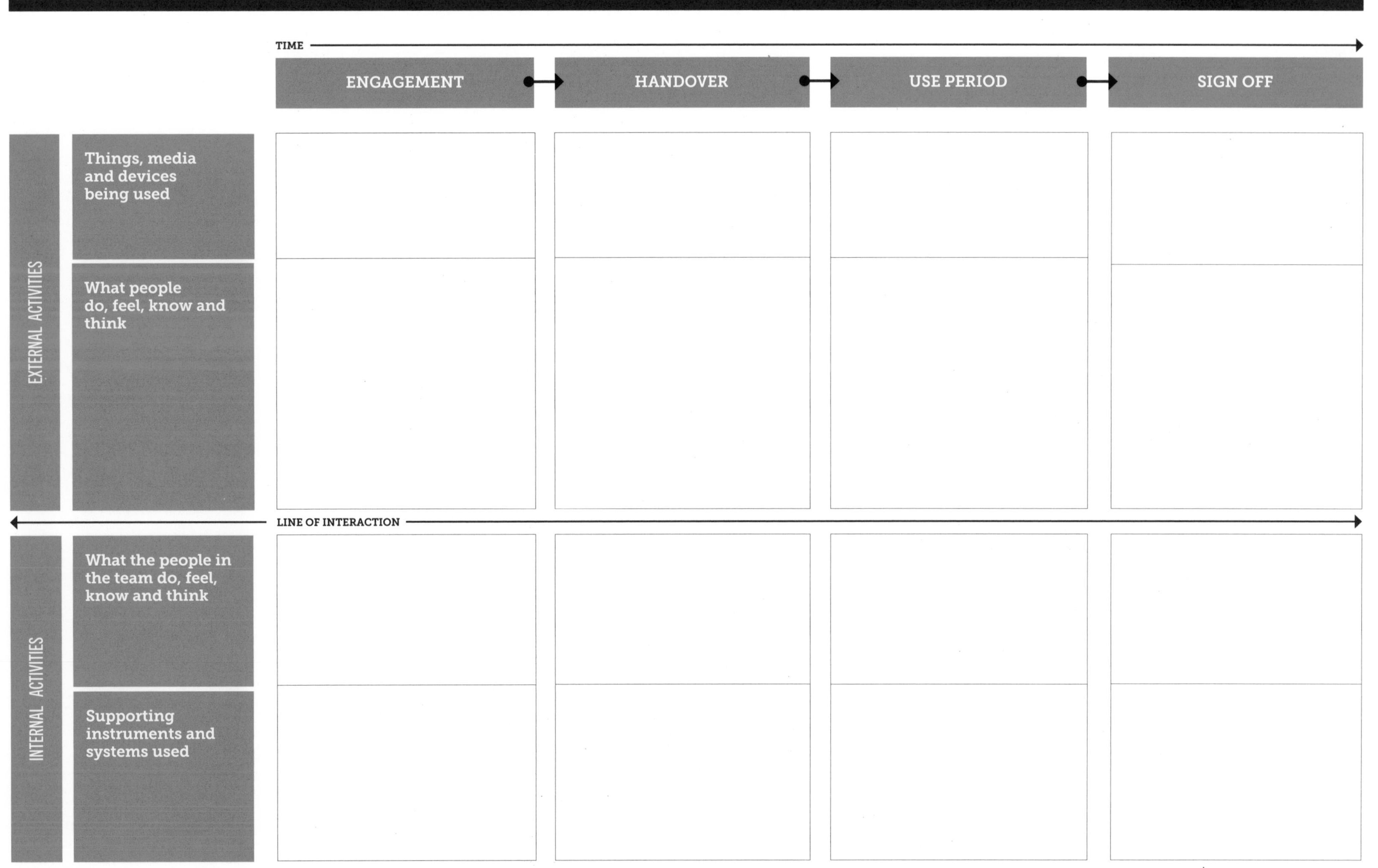

CASE STUDY

TOOL USED: PERSONAS, PROBLEM DEFINITION, IMPROVEMENT TRIGGERS

ORGANISATION: SBCSOL - INCUBADORA DE EMPREENDIMENTOS SOLIDARIOS

COUNTRY: BRAZIL

SECTOR: ENTREPRENEURSHIP AND SKILL DEVELOPMENT

ROLE: SOCIAL DESIGNER

CONTACT PERSON: RENATA MENDES

EMAIL: RENATACM@UOL.COM.BR

Despite coming from a region with such a rich history, these artisan products seem rather basic and functional and are not based on market research.

Sumaré, a city in São Paulo has a very deep history of political and community life. The city is part of a settlement won over thirty years ago by the Movimento dos Sem Terra (Landless Movement), fighting for agrarian reform in Brazil. I'm working with a group of 5 women farmers who make crafts with banana fibre in Sumaré to develop new products, such as lampshades, mats, boxes. Despite coming from a region with such a rich history, these artisan products seem rather basic and functional and are not based on market research. Thus, even though they are technically well developed, the women have difficulty selling their current range of products.

SAMPLES OF THE BANANA FIBRE PRODUCTS MADE BY THE ARTISANS.

ADAPTED WORKSHEETS FOR PROBLEM DEFINITION AND IMPROVEMENT TRIGGERS TRANSLATED IN THE LOCAL LANGUAGE WERE USED IN CO-CREATION WORKSHOP.

WHY WE USED THE TOOL:

We decided to work on the stage before product development i.e. analysing what these women artisans value and what their story is. We planned to use these stories to create a collection of products, giving them a strong foundation that would increase chances of better sales. We also looked at the entire supply chain - from the harvest of raw materials to the storage of products, to make it more efficient.

We adapted and used the Personas, Problem Definition and Improvement Triggers tools for this exercise. Firstly, we needed the artisans to talk about themselves and their community. Here, we used our adaptation of the Personas tool to help conduct research on the history and stories of the artisans and their community. We supplemented these stories with the main problems perceived by the artisans using the Problem Definition tool. I had adapted the Problem Definition tool to project these problems as opportunities.

For more detailed analysis and critique of the artisan's current production techniques, we used an adaptation of the tool Improvement Triggers, which presents a series of commands to help you look at the matter in a different way,

> The tool introduces the concept of 'business thinking' to people who have no prior experience as entrepreneurs.

HOW WE USED THE TOOL:

To talk about themselves, the artisans received a closed 'treasure box'. Each woman would open the box and describe what they found inside. Inside, there would be a mirror, which the women used to recognise and expose their thoughts, individual dreams and skills. Later we collated these into groups and made Personas for each group. I used an adaptation of the Personas to create a fictional character that was based on the features that artisans described. Along with this we also collected problems that they felt stood in their way. We then used the Improvement Triggers to come up with new ideas. Often many ideas would get repeated and sometimes we would mix questions - but the number of responses exhausted the number of possibilities and gave a sense of complete analysis. The lack of suitable equipment and materials in this village is very common. I couldn't print PDFs of the tool worksheets, so I redrew them in my workplace using coloured paper, post its and slate.

RESULTS OF USING THE TOOL:

The tool introduces the concept of 'business thinking' to people who have no prior experience as entrepreneurs. It helped the women farmers organise their thoughts and was instrumental in helping them construct concrete goals for themselves and detailing out activities needed for each stage.

Furthermore, the tool provided an accessible language for everyone, irrespective of their education and awareness. Guided by the questions on the canvas, we built a very solid value proposition, which guided the development of other areas of the business model.

Building a vision for a Microfinance Institution based on real life stories from its beneficiaries.

It is but seldom that an everyday experience is so profound and timely that it stirs in a person the courage to set things right.

The Story of Spandana

• Guntur Town, Andhra Pradesh, India, 1997
Padmaja Reddy was working for an NGO when one day, she saw a rag-picker woman on the street whose plight made her curious about how she could help her.

ग्रहों के प्रमुख योग

चार ग्रहों की युति का फल

"When the Rich are Too Rich

There are Ways

and When the Poor are Too Poor

There are Ways...

and That Way Will Come Soon."

I want to sustain & implement by better engaging people that can benefit from my work

▽

MARKETING MIX

INSPIRED BY
Nesta (2009) Worksheet 4a: Marketing Mix. In: Creative Enterprise Toolkit.

LEVEL OF INVOLVEMENT

REQUIRES SOME DIALOGUE with colleagues/peers. Plan for some time to interact and fill out in collaboration over a day maybe.

What is it & why should I do it?

'Marketing' what you do doesn't have to mean selling it. The Marketing Mix will help you do this, if that's your goal, but it's also useful for defining the different ways in which people might form opinions about your work - as well as highlighting opportunities for influencing this process. This is a key tool to help you get buy-in from stakeholders for your project.

The **Marketing Mix** worksheet is structured to help you examine your work from the perspective of your beneficiaries. All the elements involved somehow influence the judgements people might make about what you do, helping you understand better those areas which may need attention when trying to achieve real impact. The Marketing Mix can be useful for determining how you trigger the people you're working with, to engage with what you're trying to do.

HOW TO USE IT

Don't think of the Marketing Mix only as a commercial activity. Look at it as an opportunity to reflect on your work from the experience of a beneficiary.

This tool helps clarify their needs and experiences and helps to think of how to improve your current or future offering.

You can start filling out the different boxes in the worksheet in no particular order. Just go through each section and adapt your answers until you feel they sufficiently answer the questions posed.

Product		Place	Price
Physical Environment	Process	People	Promotion

I want to sustain and implement
by better engaging people that can benefit from my work

MARKETING MIX

Product
Describe the 'Unique Selling Proposition' that clearly states the features & benefits that make your work unique.

Place
Where is your work available to people & how does it get there?

Price
What are the returns you recieve for your work?

Physical environment
What impression does your workplace give to your audience, suppliers & staff?

Process
What are the procedures that your company uses to deliver your work?

People
Which of your staff or representatives are involved?

Promotion
What are your means to make your audience aware of your work?

Building multi-stakeholders workflows to understand connections and create opportunities within the public health system.

I want to sustain & implement by executing my plan without being overwhelmed

CRITICAL TASKS LIST

INSPIRED BY
Nesta (2009) Worksheet 4b: Critical Marketing Tasks. In: Creative Enterprise Toolkit.

LEVEL OF INVOLVEMENT

REQUIRES SOME DIALOGUE with colleagues/peers. Plan for some time to interact and fill out in collaboration over a day maybe.

What is it & why should I do it?

The **Critical Tasks List** is a way to ensure that what you set out to do is actually possible within the timeframe and budget you have available. This is useful when working alone, but becomes even more important when you need to focus and align your work with others. The list provides a common reference point which everyone can use to keep track of how things are progressing. This enables you to manage your projects by focusing on the tasks at hand.

It's a simple thing to do - and taking the time to do it can really help when you're in danger of being overwhelmed by the amount of work that needs to be done, or worried about how exactly an idea is going to be implemented. When your work starts to grow, and tasks start being shared amongst a large group of people, you may want to shift to a more dynamic and professional project management tool. The Critical Task list is a first step to develop a routine in organising your ongoing work.

HOW TO USE IT

List all the activities to be carried out, together with who they are assigned to, the budget available, the deadline for completion and the process for final sign off.

Don't fear specificity. Deliberate the activity with the people assigned to it and add in as much detail as possible. You can also break up specific roles people play to perform a specific activity.

You should regularly monitor and review the progress of your critica tasks, both in terms of staff resources and budgets. Any deviatio from the plan should be acted upon or agreed and amended.

I want to sustain and implement
by executing my plan without being overwhelmed

CRITICAL TASKS LIST

ACTIVITY	ASSIGNED TO	BUDGET	DEADLINE	SIGN OFF

Presenting a plan for a business around farming practices and methods in urban contexts.

I want to sustain & implement launching or growing what I do

BUSINESS PLAN

INSPIRED BY
Gov.uk (2013) Write a Business Plan.

LEVEL OF INVOLVEMENT

REQUIRES SOME DIALOGUE with colleagues/peers. Plan for some time to interact and fill out in collaboration over a day maybe.

What is it & why should I do it?

A **Business Plan** is a structured description of how you do what you do. The plan needs to articulate the problem the business proposes to solve, a vision for how that will be accomplished, and what uniquely qualifies you to do that. Writing a Business Plan is often essential when trying to convince potential funders who want to know where their money will be going. The plan should also include an introduction to the management team, a marketing plan, an operations and financial plan, and any other requirements. This means covering all the different aspects that a funding partner might be interested in, using the kind of language they will be looking out for.

While a tool like the Business Model Canvas provides an overview of what you want to do (as well as why and how you want to do it), a Business Plan is a way of providing more detail on the operational and economic foundation of how you will make this a reality. The structured worksheet of the Business Plan helps you describe what makes your idea for social impact a viable endeavour.

HOW TO USE IT

This worksheet points out the key aspects that you need to keep in mind as you develop your Business Plan.

It is easiest to first write a quick draft of your Business Plan and then keep re-writing. Don't spend too long getting the draft and even the next versions 'just right' because it is very likely you will re-write the plan numerous times. During the process you'll come up with much better ways of explaining of what makes your idea for social good feasible.

Writing up the business overview is a good place to start. This includes a few paragraphs about the main idea, the need and market for it. This will be followed up by your plan for action and what makes your team strong for this task. While approaching funders or donors, a key component of the Business Plan is to have a clear statement of why you need the money, how the money will be spent and how it can be earned back.

An important element in the Business Plan is the executive summary. This usually sits at the start of the document, but it is seldom written as the first section. It is easier to write it after you have completed a first draft of your Business Plan.

Once you've written your Business Plan, get someone to read it for you. It helps to get a fresh perspective to identify any issues you might have missed out on.

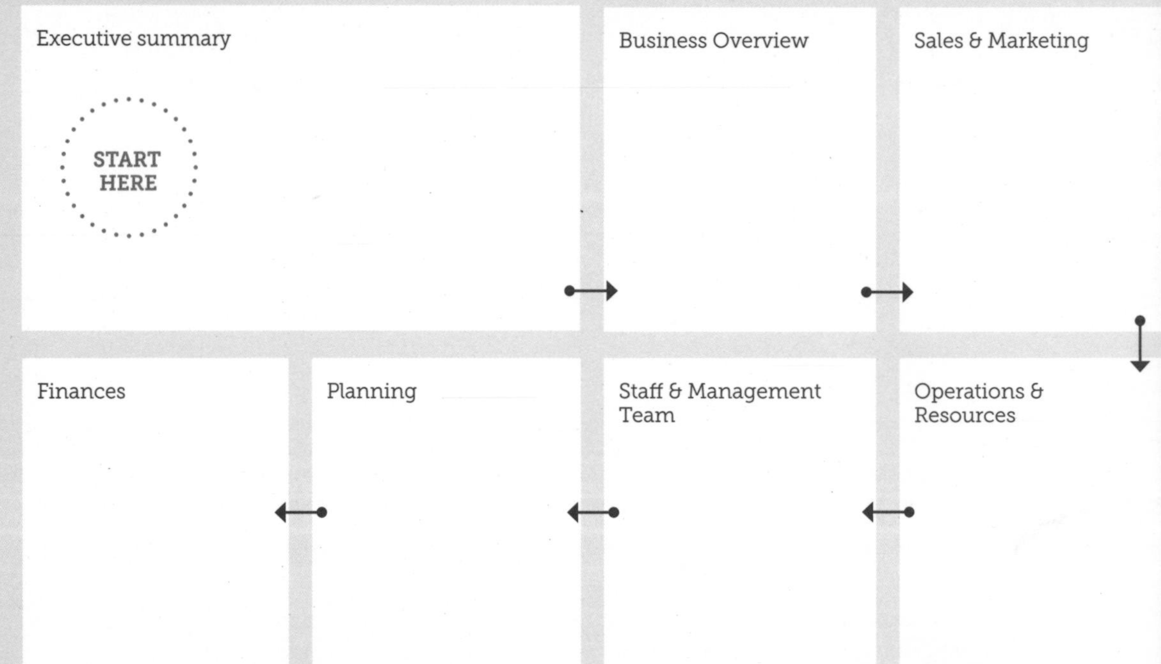

I want to sustain and implement
by launching or growing what I do

BUSINESS PLAN

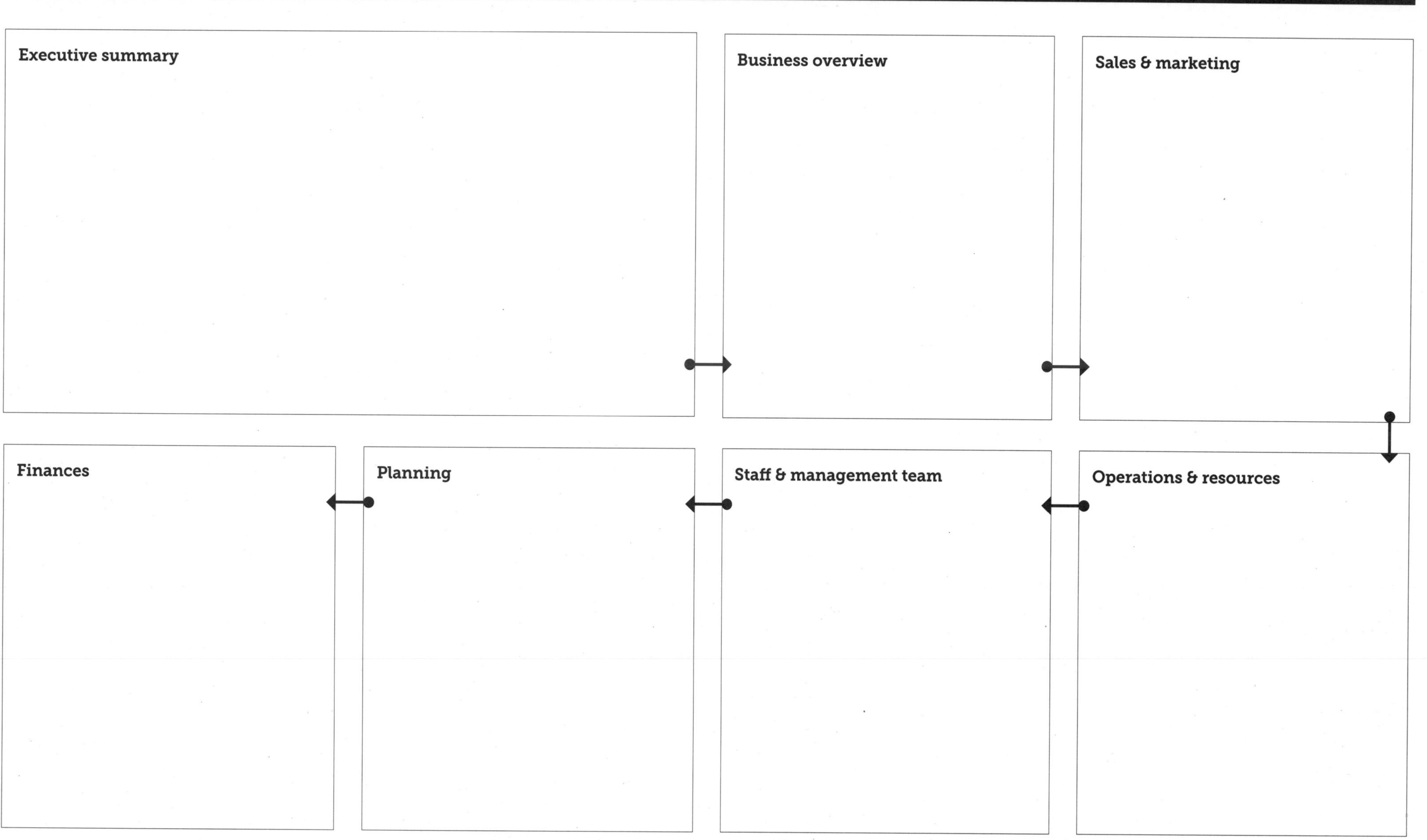

Mapping a pathway to scale an urban slums sanitation project.

I want to sustain & implement while exploring different ways of increasing the scale of my work

SCALING PLAN

INSPIRED BY

Ali R., Mulgan G., Halkett R., Sanders B. (2007) In and out of sync: The challenge of growing social innovations. London, Nesta.

LEVEL OF INVOLVEMENT

MORE COMPLEX TOOL that should ideally be done over a few days. Given the strategic nature of the inputs/outputs, this needs consultations with seniors, peers and ideally needs to be revised after a first pass.

What is it & why should I do it?

Once a project or pilot has been successfully implemented, the next step is to build upon this success by sustaining and growing it further. Essentially this means extending the reach of your work to a bigger population. There are many ways of scaling up - from replicating the project across geographies, to collaborating with different organisations towards a shared vision, or even expanding upon the problem your work addresses.

Social organisations can face quite a few challenges in scaling up their work: keeping a clear focus (e.g. strategic spread rather than just sprawling out); negotiating cost structures and revenues (e.g. sustainable income rather than one-of grants or capital); handling effective supply and demand (e.g. demonstrable results, at the right costs, for a receptive audience); leading organisational change (e.g. founders are replaced by managers); choosing the right organisational form (e.g. grow the organisation, partner, merge, take over, license, franchise). There are several resources that need to be in place for a pilot project to be scaled without compromising the necessary impact it must have. Regardless of how and when you decide to scale, it is key to first build a shared vision for scaling within your organisation. The **Scaling Plan** aims to stimulate serious dialogue about this with key internal and external stakeholders.

HOW TO USE IT

The worksheet helps developing a shared vision on scaling up, while assessing your resources and whether your organisation is ready to take the next step. Based on the assessment of the situation, you can decide your readiness to scale, what aspects need strengthening and what aspects need more work.

The worksheet can be used in a workshop with team members from your organisation, potential donors or even the intended beneficiaries and other stakeholders. It shows five key areas which you should consider to analyse whether your organisation is ready to scale. Use the questions on the worksheet as prompts to have a critical in-depth conversation on what you are certain about and what needs further investigation.

While filling out the worksheet, try to give evidence in the form of factual data, rather than just anecdotes. It often helps to collect some of this evidence in advance of the meeting.

Try to be as open, thorough and self-critical as possible. The more detailed answers you give, the deeper your understanding of the situation will be.

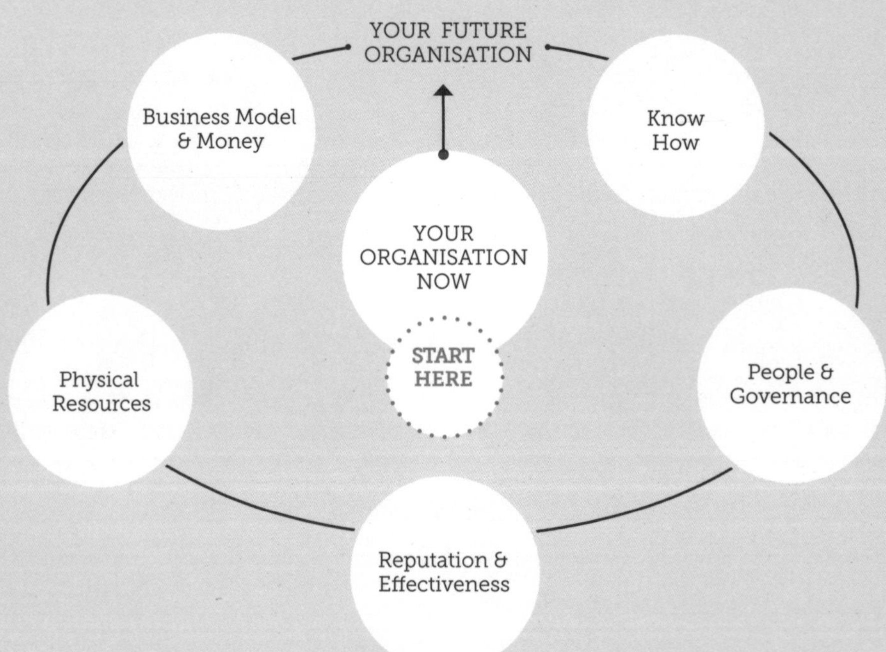

I want to sustain and implement
while exploring different ways of increasing the scale of my work

SCALING PLAN

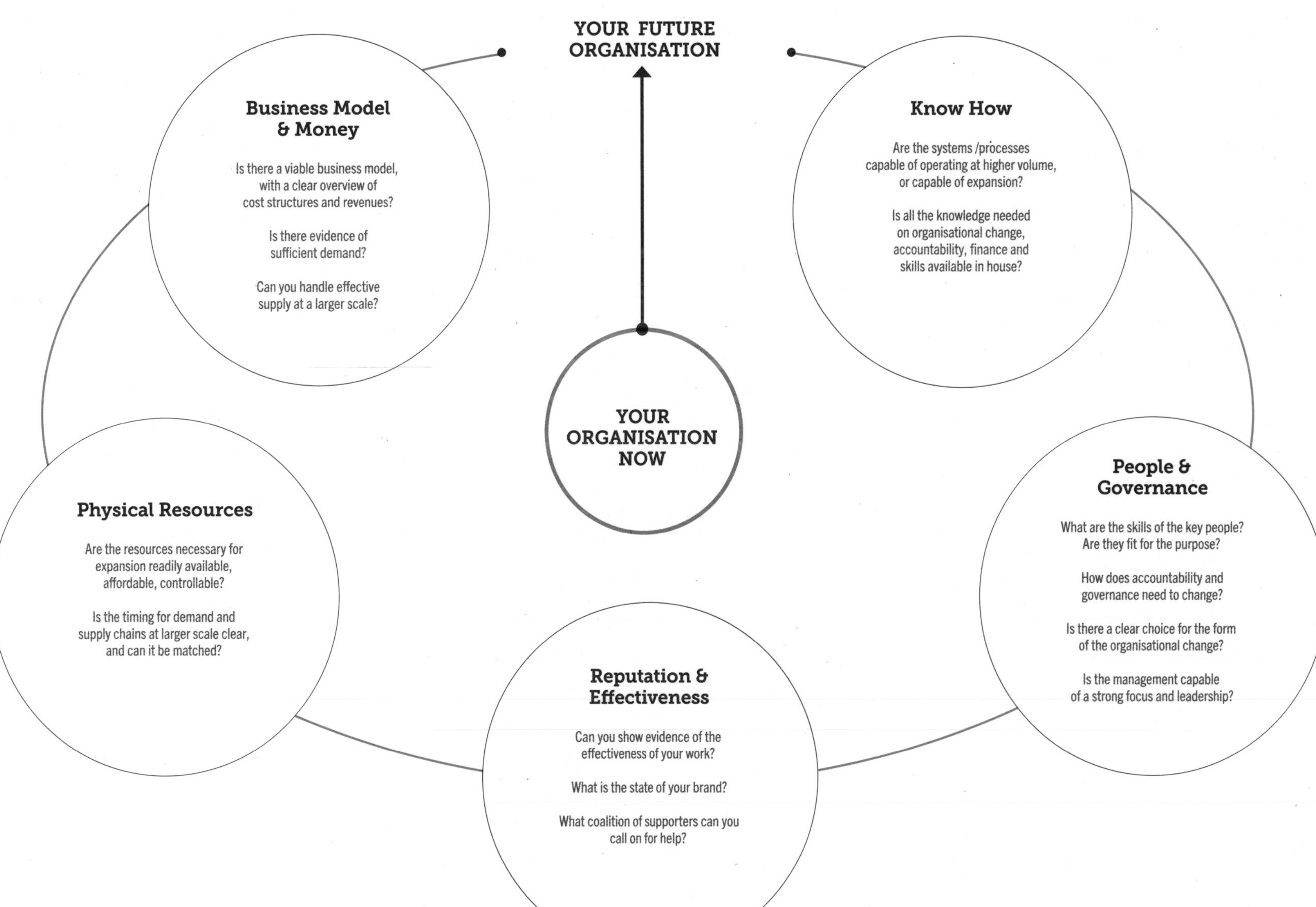

CASE STUDY

TOOL USED: SWOT ANALYSIS , QUESTION LADDER AND CRITICAL TASKS LIST

ORGANISATION: MP TECHNICAL ASSISTANCE AND SUPPORTIVE TEAM (MPTAST)

COUNTRY: INDIA

SECTOR: PUBLIC HEALTH, NUTRITION AND WASH

ROLE: DISTRICT PROJECT CO-ODINATOR

CONTACT PERSON: RAVI KOMMURI

EMAIL: RKOMMURI@MPTAST.ORG

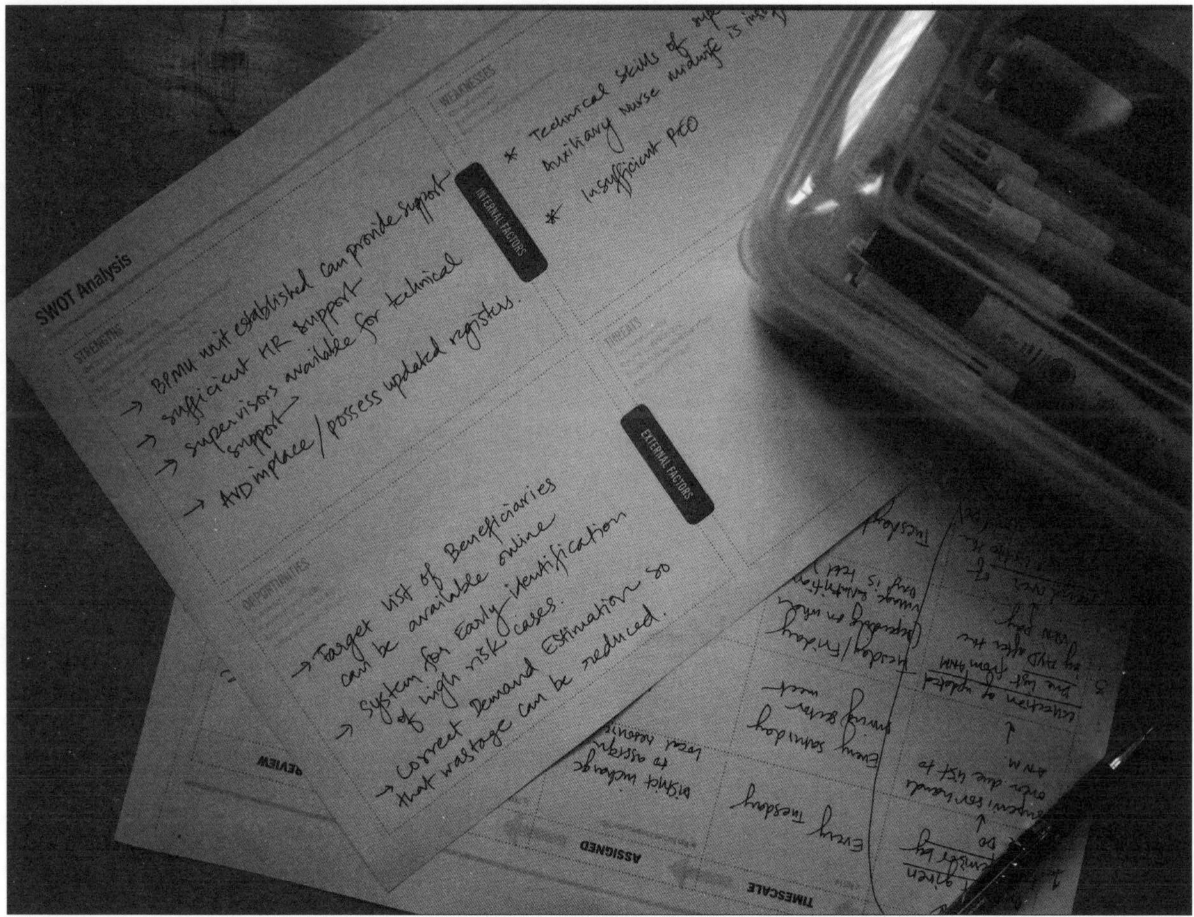

THE WORKSHEETS JOINTLY CREATED TO ASSESS THE TEAMS CURRENT WEAKNESSES AND WAYS TO OVERCOME THEM.

Madhya Pradesh, a state in central India has very high infant and mother mortality rates, compared to the national average.

Our programme helps strengthen the system and we work closely with the Health Department, WCD (Women & Child Development) & PHED (Public Health Engineering Department) departments aiming to reduce MMR (Maternal Mortality Ratio), IMR (Infant Mortality Ratio), Malnutrition & TFR (Total Fertility Rate) in the state of Madhya Pradesh in India.

MCTS (Mother & Child Tracking System) is an online monitoring software which has been developed by Government of India with an objective to track the different services being provided/ to be provided to a pregnant mother right from conception until the baby turns a year old. This tracking of service delivery plays a vital role and helps in guiding and planning towards the actions to be taken towards MMR & IMR.

The tracking system still needs to be worked upon further before it can be implemented.

WHY WE USED THE TOOL:

My team mates and I used the Theory of Change and Causes Diagram in one combination, and SWOT Analysis, Question Ladder and the Critical Tasks list in another combination. Our aim is to strengthen the usage of the MCTS software by re-defining roles, incentives and contingency strategies for all the people and stakeholders responsible for its functioning. We did this by using a set of tools to re-visit and consolidate the challenge we are facing, and then use another set of tools to identify potential team members and create a critical pathway to implement our solution.

HOW WE USED THE TOOL:

We used these tools in Jabalpur District in Madhya Pradesh as a pilot. First, I explained the purpose of doing the whole exercise to the field team - the District Health Officer, the Auxiliary Nurse Midwife (ANM) and the Accredited Social Health Assistant (ASHA) worker.

We took stock of :

1. Why the MCTS system is not being updated at all;
2. The people involved and what their roles are, and;
3. Understanding the bottlenecks that we should address to solve the issue.

We then used a combination of SWOT Analysis, Question Ladder and Critical Tasks list.

SWOT ANALYSIS

To understand the team's strengths & weaknesses, to help us figure out what they can do to be more efficient and help people take responsibility for their actions.

QUESTION LADDER

To help redefine individual responsibilities with the entire team's consensus and input.

CRITICAL TASKS LIST

To help develop timelines to put the new plan into place.

RESULTS OF USING THE TOOL:

The SWOT Analysis helped the team review their strengths and helped us understand how individual contributions affect the team's work and vice versa. It also helped us envisage possible 'threats' that could hamper the smooth functioning of the system - something that we had never considered before.

The Question Ladder helped us identify potential team members that could be re-assigned with new tasks, timelines and accomplishments in the updated system. The process was participatory and had the consensus of all those involved directly and indirectly.

For us, developing or improving programmes and measuring outcomes go hand in hand.

We used the Critical Tasks List to create a new schedule for the updating the service system and create markers to receive feedback on how effective the new system is. In every pilot it is critical to measure the 'perceived and actual' change before we can even think of scaling up. The task list helped us chart that critical journey and milestones for the pilot.

Bird's Eye View on Social Innovation

The Development Impact and You toolkit has been specially designed for practitioners to dive straight into action. The tools presented here are grounded in existing theories and practices of innovation, design, and business development.

This chapter offers a 'bird's eye view' of the main pillars underlying the theory and management of social innovation and each topic is supplemented with references for further reading.

01 Stages of Innovation

Innovation is sometimes written about as an almost magical process. But it is wrong to see innovation as a mystery. It is true that innovation is rarely simple or predictable, but looking closely at what actually happens, it is also true that the overall innovation process is structured and systematic.

Although every real innovation is a complex story of loops and jumps, there are various stages that most innovations pass through. This framework is useful for understanding how to put ideas to work, and focusing on the different methods, and different mindset, needed at each stage.

THE SEVEN STAGES ARE:

Opportunities & challenges

These include all the initiating factors like a crisis, new evidence, inspirations etc. which highlight the need for change. This might involve diagnosing the root causes of a problem, or identifying the opportunities that a new change could bring about.

Generating ideas

Most of the ideas you come up with at first won't work. But it's only through the process of constant idea creation that you arrive at something that is radical and transformative. Use creative methods like design to increase the number of solution options from a wide range of sources.

Developing & testing

New ideas are always helped by robust criticism. It is through trial and error that ideas are iterated and strengthened. This can be done by simply trying things out, or through more rigorous prototyping and randomised controlled trials.

Making the case

Before you try to implement your idea, you need to prove that it can work and is better than what is already there. Build up firm evidence to back it up and then share it honestly.

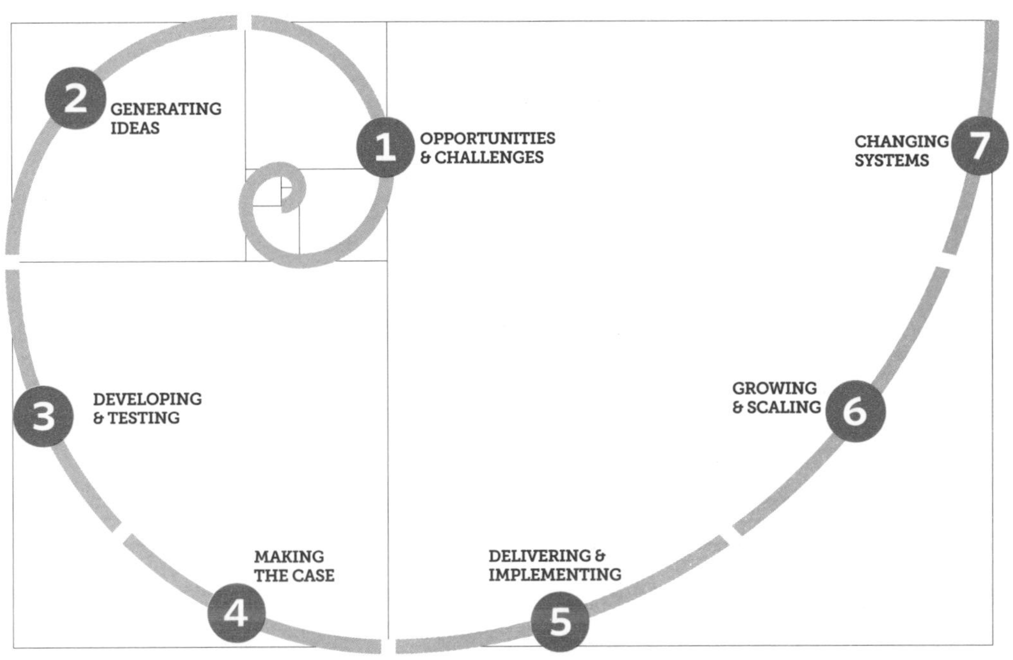

Delivering & implementing

This is when the solution becomes everyday practice. It includes identifying what is working well, and what is not, as well as securing income streams that enable the long term financial sustainability to carry the innovation forward.

Growing & scaling

In this stage there are a range of strategies for growing and spreading an innovation - from organisational growth, to licensing and franchising. Emulation and inspiration also play a critical role in spreading an idea or practice in a more organic and adaptive manner.

Changing systems

Systemic innovation is where maximum social impact can be created. It usually involves changes in the public and private sector over long periods of time, and the interaction of many elements and new ways of thinking.

Further reading on the stages of innovation:

- Caulier-Grice J., Mulgan G., Murray R., (2010) Open Book of Social Innovation. London, The Young Foundation, Nesta & The Lab. Available online from: http://www.nesta.org.uk/library/documents/Social_Innovator_020310.pdf
- Nesta (2013) Available online from: http://www.nesta.org.uk/develop-your-skills

02 Use of evidence

Have a plan for building evidence from the outset of your project. All innovators, commissioners, service users and investors need evidence to know whether the products or services they develop, buy or invest in make a positive difference. In fields such as medicine, using evidence is much more common and offers interesting opportunities to learn from. The main benefit of regular and systematic reviewing of evidence is that it enables a more effective way to use data or information to test assumptions, continually improve, and create a more sustained impact.

Using evidence as a natural part of projects and decision making should be common practice for organisations. And not just evidence on your current projects: understanding what has worked before, and awareness of what works in the wider landscape makes it easier to evaluate and replicate success. The following page has is a useful framework that Nesta has developed to show the different standards of evidence that you should aim to build up throughout a project to show that it is making a difference.

THE FIVE LEVELS ARE:

❶ Account of impact

A clear explanation of what the new or improved product or service does and how it could have impact on your intended outcome, and why that would be an improvement on the current situation.

❷ Correlation

Observation of some positive impact happening on the part of the users of the product or service, but no confirmation yet on what caused this. You might conduct pre and post survey evaluations, or a cohort/panel study for instance.

❸ Causation

Establishment of evidence of positive change amongst the users of the product or service due to the product or service. Think about how to isolate the impact of the product or service through a control group selected randomly to strengthen your evidence base.

❹ Independent replication

Independent validation of the positive outcomes of the product or service, with the aim to deliver this positive impact at a reasonable cost in other places, such as commercial standards or industry kitemarks.

❺ Scaled

Use methods like multiple replication evaluations or future scenario analysis to generate clear and tested evidence that the product or service can been delivered at multiple locations and delivers a strong, positive impact, whilst remaining a financially viable proposition.

	1	2	3	4	5
LEVELS OF EVIDENCE	you can describe what you do and why it matters logically, coherently and convincingly	you capture data that shows positive change, but you cannot confirm that your intervention caused the change	you can demonstrate causality with reference to a control group or comparison group	you have one or more independent evaluations that confirms your conclusions and potentially replicates your results	you have manuals, systems and procedures to support and ensure faithful replication of your innovation
HOW TO GENERATE THE EVIDENCE	you should be able to do this yourself by drawing on existing data and research from other sources. Constructing a theory of change should help you to logically and coherently describe how your intervention will achieve the effects you outline.	at this stage, data can begin to show the effect your innovation has but may not demonstrate direct casuality. Many of the methods outlined in the previous topic will help as would more structured surveys of your participants before and after, or at intervals during your invention.	in order to demonstrate casuality, you will need to show evidence of what happened to those involved in your intervention alongside evidence of what happened to a similar group who were not involved in your intervention (called a control group). Selecting participants randomly to both groups strengthens your evidence and you will need to have a sufficiently large sample for your results to be convincing.	you should commission a robust independent evaluation that demonstrates and validates why and how your innovation creates impact. You might also seek endorsement via commercial standards, industry kitemarks or similar.	you need to show that your product or service can be operated by someone else, somewhere else, whilst continuing to have positive direct impact on the outcome and remaining a financially viable proposition. Towards this end, you might pursue an evaluation across multiple contexts that, amongst other things, tests the fidelity of practice and outcomes between sites.

Further reading on evidence:

- Puttick R. (2011) Ten Steps to Transform the Use of Evidence. London, Nesta. Available online from:http://www.nesta.org.uk/library/documents/TenStepsBlog.pdf
- Ludlow J., Puttick R. (2012) Standards of Evidence. London, Nesta. Available online from:http://www.nesta.org.uk/publications/nesta-standards-evidence
- Mulgan G., Puttick R. (2013) Making Evidence Useful: The Case for New Institutions. London, Nesta. Available online from: http://www.nesta.org.uk/library/documents/MakingEvidenceUseful.pdf
- DfID: Department for International Development (2013) How to note. London, Dfid. Available online from: http://bit.ly/dfid-evidence
- BOND for International Development (2013) Evidence Principles. London, BOND. Available online from: http://www.bond.org.uk/effectiveness/principles#download

03 Scaling Up

The concept of scaling up is attracting increasing attention as it extends the reach of innovative pilot projects to large populations. There are many ways of scaling up – from repeating an idea in a different place, or collaborating with different organisations and building relationships that work.

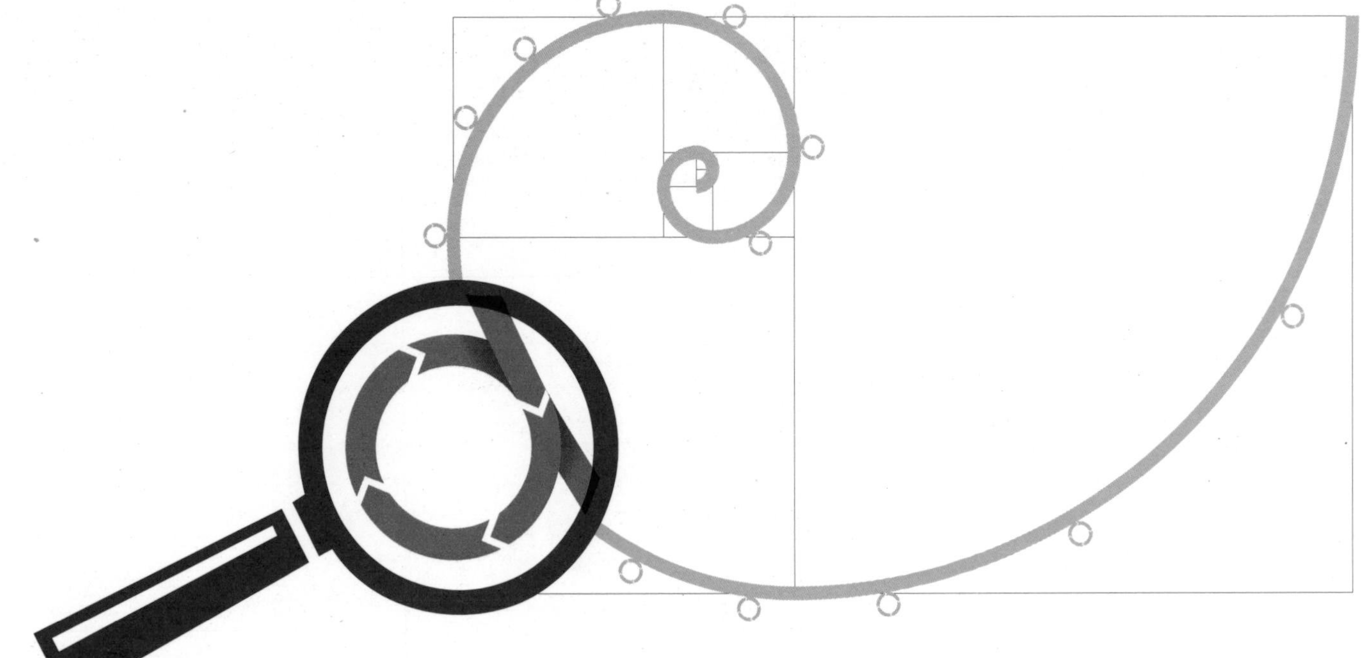

To determine if a project is ready to scale and achieve greater impact in a more widespread manner, it is important to find the things that work, get them to work smoothly and move them up to the next level. It is useful to think through effective demand and effective supply; i.e. is there someone out there who is willing to pay for your idea? And does your idea work, and does it work better than the alternatives? Nearly always the task of scaling a social idea involves increasing both effective supply and effective demand, but your strategy will vary greatly depending on which comes first.

From a distance great innovations may look like radical leaps. But from close up they often turn out to be made of small steps that build on each other to achieve bigger scale. Under a microscope the different stages of innovation might be magnified to show 'mini-spiral' processes taking place - individual projects that an organisation might be developing to support the overall innovation process.

Further reading on scaling up:

- Ali R., Mulgan G., Halkett R., Sanders B. (2007) In and out of sync: The challenge of growing social innovations. London, Nesta. Available online from:http://www.nesta.org.uk/publications/and-out-sync
- Cooley L., Kohl R. (2006) Scaling Up - From Vision to Large-scale Change: A Management Framework for Practitioners. Washington, Management Systems Institute, John D. and Catherine T. MacArthur Foundation. Available online from: http://www.msiworldwide.com/wp-content/uploads/Scaling-Up-Framework.pdf

04 Systems thinking

The word 'system' refers to complex and interdependent infrastructures, rules and patterns in our societies and economies. Changes in one part may affect other parts, so complex issues require changes and innovations across the system.

Systems thinking brings together the different elements and innovations that achieve a common purpose. A single organisation almost never has all the skills and resources to provide the full range of activities that are needed to create a big impact. This means that an innovation resulting in systemic change almost always involves an alliance of partners, suppliers and distributors, supported by networks, clubs, think tanks and development agencies.

Further reading on systems thinking:

- Leadbeater C., Mulgan G. (2013) Systems Innovation Discussion Paper. London, Nesta. Available online from: http://www.nesta.org.uk/library/documents/Systemsinnovationv8.pdf
- Seddon J. (2013) Systems failure and Systems thinking. London, Nesta. Available online from: http://www.nesta.org.uk/blogs/systemic_innovation_a_discussion_series/systems_failure_and_systems_thinking

Key Sources of Inspiration

01 INNOVATION FLOWCHART
Nesta (2013) Innovation Flowchart. Available online from: http://www.nesta.org.uk/publications/innovation-flowchart

02 EVIDENCE PLANNING
Nesta (2009) Worksheet 2b: Evidence Modelling. In: Creative Enterprise Toolkit. Available online from: http://www.nesta.org.uk/publications/creative-enterprise-toolkit

03 SWOT ANALYSIS
MindTools (1996) SWOT Analysis. Available online from: http://www.mindtools.com/pages/article/newTMC_05.htm

04 BUSINESS MODEL CANVAS
Osterwalder A., Pigneur Y (2010) Business Model Generation. Available online from: http://www.businessmodelgeneration.com/downloads/business_model_canvas_poster.pdf

05 BUILDING PARTNERSHIPS MAP
Tennyson R. (2003) 12 Phases in the Partnering Process, p4. In: The Partnering Toolbook. Available online from: http://www.toolkitsportdevelopment.org/html/resources/E1/E1585B25-8A8A-44A9-BC6C-F519987AD2CE/pt-en.pdf

06 LEARNING LOOP
IDEO (2011) Deliver: Create a learning plan, p145. In: IDEO, Human Centered Design Toolkit. Edition - 2. London: IDEO. Available online from: http://www.ideo.com/work/human-centered-design-toolkit/

07 EXPERIENCE TOUR
Design Council (2011) Service Safari. In: Keeping Connected Design Challenge. Available online from: https://www.hvcollege.com/documents/technology/ServiceSafariActivity.pdf

08 PROBLEM DEFINITION
Julier J., Kimbell L. (2012) Problem Definition. p30. In: The Social Design Methods Menu. Available online from: http://www.lucykimbell.com/stuff/Fieldstudio_SocialDesignMethodsMenu.pdf

09 CAUSES DIAGRAM
Namahn and Yellow Window Service Design, Design Flanders (2012) Cause Diagram. In: Service design toolkit. Available online from: http://www.servicedesigntoolkit.org/assets/posters/workposter_causediagram_a1.pdf

10 THEORY OF CHANGE
Nesta (2011) Theory of Change. Available online from: http://www.nesta.org.uk/library/documents/TheoryOfChangeDiagram_Editable.pdf

11 SHADOWING
Lovlie L.,Reason B.,Polaine A. (2013) Service Design: From Insight to Implementation. p54-p57. Rosenfeld Media

12 INTERVIEW GUIDE
IDEO, Bill & Melinda Gates Foundation (2012) Develop an interview approach p58. In: Human Centred Design Toolkit. Available online from: http://www.hcdconnect.org/methods/interview-techniques

13 QUESTION LADDER
Teachers College Columbia University (2012) Question. In: Social Innovation Toolkit. Available online from: http://www.socialinnovationtoolkit.com/question.html

14 STORYWORLD
Julier J., Kimbell L. (2012) Storyworld. p24. In: The Social Design Methods Menu. Available online from: http://www.lucykimbell.com/stuff/Fieldstudio_SocialDesignMethodsMenu.pdf

15 PEOPLE & CONNECTIONS MAP
Namahn and Yellow Window Service Design, Design Flanders (2012) Stakeholder Mapping. In: Service design toolkit. Available online from: http://www.servicedesigntoolkit.org/assets/posters/workposter_stakeholdermapping_a1.pdf

16 TARGET GROUP
Nesta (2009) Worksheet 3a: Your Customers. In: Creative Enterprise Toolkit. Available online from: http://www.nesta.org.uk/publications/creative-enterprise-toolkit

17 PERSONAS
Business Design Toolkit (2010) Personas. Available online from: http://www.businessdesigntools.com/2011/12/personas/

18 PROMISES & POTENTIAL MAP
IDEO (2011) Deliver: Plan a pipeline of solutions, p135. In: IDEO, Human Centered Design Toolkit. Edition - 2. London: IDEO. Available online from: http://www.ideo.com/work/human-centered-design-toolkit/

19 CREATIVE WORKSHOP
Lovlie L.,Reason B.,Polaine A. (2013) Service Design: From Insight to Implementation. p60. Rosenfeld Media

20 FAST IDEA GENERATOR
Nesta (2013) Fast Idea Generator. Available online from: http://www.nesta.org.uk/publications/fast-idea-generator

21 THINKING HATS
de Bono, E. (1985) Six Thinking Hats. USA: Little, Brown and Company. Available online from: http://www.debonogroup.com/six_thinking_hats.php

22 VALUE MAPPING
Nesta (2009) Worksheet 2a: Your Values. In: Creative Enterprise Toolkit. Available online from: http://www.nesta.org.uk/publications/creative-enterprise-toolkit

23 IMPROVEMENT TRIGGERS
Eberle, B (1997) Scamper Worksheet. USA: Prufrock Press. Available online from: http://bmgi.org/tools-templates/scamper-worksheet

24 PROTOTYPE TESTING PLAN
Nesta (2011) Prototyping in Public Spaces. Available online from: http://www.nesta.org.uk/publications/prototyping-public-services

25 EXPERIENCE MAP
Schneider J., Stickdorn M., (2010)The Customer Journey Canvas. In: This is Service Design Thinking. Amsterdam: BIS Publishers. Available online from: http://files.thisisservicedesignthinking.com/tisdt_cujoca.pdf

26 BLUEPRINT
Julier J., Kimbell L. (2012) Blueprint. p44. In: The Social Design Methods Menu. Available online from: http://www.lucykimbell.com/stuff/Fieldstudio_SocialDesignMethodsMenu.pdf

27 MARKETING MIX
Nesta (2009) Worksheet 4a: Marketing Mix. In: Creative Enterprise Toolkit. Available online from: http://www.nesta.org.uk/publications/creative-enterprise-toolkit

28 CRITICAL TASKS LIST
Nesta (2009) Worksheet 4b: Critical Marketing Tasks. In: Creative Enterprise Toolkit. Available online from: http://www.nesta.org.uk/publications/creative-enterprise-toolkit

29 BUSINESS PLAN
Gov.uk (2013) Write a Business Plan. Available online from: https://www.gov.uk/write-business-plan

30 SCALING PLAN
http://www.nesta.org.uk/publications/and-out-sync

Recommended Resources

PUBLICATIONS

1. Aid on the Edge of Chaos
   Ben Ramalingam
2. Dead Aid
   Dambisa Moyo
3. Poor Economics: A Radical Rethinking of the Way to Fight Global Poverty
   Esther Duflo & Abhijit Banerjee
4. Creating a World without poverty: Social Business and the Future of Capitalism
   Muhamad Yunus
5. More Than Good Intentions: Improving the Ways the World's Poor Borrow, Save, Farm, Learn, and Stay Healthy
   Dean Karlan & Jacob Appel
6. The Power of Positive Deviance
   Richard Pascale, Jerry Sternin & Monique Sternin
7. Scaling Up – From Vision to Large-scale change: A Management Framework for Practitioners
   Larry Cooley and Richard Kohl
8. UNDP: Financing for Development
   http://www.undp.org/content/dam/undp/library/Poverty%20Reduction/Development%20Cooperation%20and%20Finance/InnovativeFinancing_Web%20ver.pdf
9. World Bank: Innovation Policy - A Guide for Developing Countries
   https://openknowledge.worldbank.org/bitstream/handle/10986/2460/548930PUB0EPI11C10Disclosed061312010.pdf?sequence=1
10. OECD: Innovation for Development
   http://www.oecd.org/sti/inno/50586251.pdf
11. Open Book of Social Innovation
   Robin Murray, Julie Caulier-Grice, Geoff Mulgan
   http://www.nesta.org.uk/publications/open-book-social-innovation
12. In and out of sync
   Nesta (Geoff Mulgan with Rushanara Ali, Richard Halkett and Ben Sanders)
   http://www.nesta.org.uk/publications/and-out-sync
13. Our Frugal Future: Lessons from India's Innovation system
   Nesta (Kirsten Bound & Ian Thornton) http://www.nesta.org.uk/publications/our-frugal-future-lessons-india%C2%92s-innovation-system
14. China's Absorptive State: Innovation and research in China
   Nesta (Kirsten Bound, Tom Saunders, James Wilsdon and Jonathan Adams) http://www.nesta.org.uk/publications/chinas-absorptive-state-innovation-and-research-china
15. The Digital Social Innovation Report
   Nesta (Nesta (Francesca Bria)
   http://s3-eu-west-1.amazonaws.com/digitalsocialinnovation/attachments/52ebbc3a72b09eaa31000001/DSI-report_(2).pdf?1391180858

WEBSITES

1. World Bank Institute
   http://wbi.worldbank.org/wbi/
   (also see World Bank Challenge Platform https://wbchallenge.imaginatik.com/, World Bank Development Marketplace http://wbi.worldbank.org/wbdm/, Innovative Solutions http://wbi.worldbank.org/wbi/approach/innovation)

2. OECD Wikiprogress
   http://www.wikiprogress.org/index.php/Wikiprogress.org:About

3. Oxfam Policy & Practice
   http://policy-practice.oxfam.org.uk/

4. ODI Publications
   http://www.odi.org.uk/publications

5. Abdul Latif Jameel Poverty Action Lab
   http://www.povertyactionlab.org/about-j-pal

TOOLKITS

1. IDEO HCD toolkit
   http://www.ideo.com/work/human-centered-design-toolkit/

2. Project Innovation
   http://www.socialinnovationtoolkit.com/home.html

3. UNICEF Innovation Labs – A Do-It-Yourself Guide
   http://www.unicefinnovationlabs.org/

4. Finding What Works
   http://findingwhatworks.org/

5. +Acumen
   http://plusacumen.org/

6. Business Model Canvas
   http://www.businessmodelgeneration.com/canvas

NETWORKS

1. Social Innovation Exchange (SIX)
   http://www.socialinnovationexchange.org/

2. Alliance for Useful Evidence
   http://www.alliance4usefulevidence.org/

3. Smart Citizen
   http://forum.smartcitizen.me/

4. Arduino
   http://arduino.cc/

5. D-Lab: International Development Innovation Network
   http://d-lab.mit.edu/idin)

6. Random Hacks of Kindness
   http://www.rhok.org/

BLOGS

1. Poverty Matters
   http://www.theguardian.com/global-development/poverty-matters

2. Chris Blattman
   http://chrisblattman.com/

3. From Poverty to Power
   http://oxfamblogs.org/fp2p/

4. DFID Bloggers
   http://blogs.dfid.gov.uk/

5. ODI Opinion
   http://www.odi.org.uk/opinion

WWW.DIYTOOLKIT.ORG

Development Impact & You

PRACTICAL TOOLS TO TRIGGER & SUPPORT SOCIAL INNOVATION

Printed in India at Gondals Press India Ltd.